EXPLORING HISTORIC WILTSHIRE
Volume 1: North

Reviews of the two volumes of *Exploring Historic Wiltshire*:

'One of the joys of walking is to discover a scene so satisfying that you know it will give pleasure for the rest of your life. And one of the delights of reading is to come upon a book that guarantees a permanent enrichment. Ken Watts has increased our chance of finding the first of these joys, and certainly provided the second, in these two recently published books... so agreeable is the style that the text reads as if a good friend is walking beside you, pointing at views, passing on anecdotes, and with the modesty of true scholarship sharing a depth of knowledge that comes from a lifetime of heartfelt enthusiasm... Ken Watts expresses this wholeness of the experience with inspiring enthusiasm... For walkers in this county, and anyone else interested in the open spaces and habitations of Wiltshire, these are major books, offering life-long reward.'

David Churchill in the *Wiltshire Gazette and Herald*

'The two volumes of *Exploring Historic Wiltshire* are... the best guides of this kind currently available which cover the county... the text also emphasises the broad sense of landscape continuity evident throughout Wiltshire and makes the two volumes a pleasure to read cover-to-cover as well as use 'in the field'... both volumes of *Exploring Historic Wiltshire* stand apart as first-class examples of a local guidebook written by a man 'in the know".'

Neil Mortimer in *3rd Stone, the Magazine for the New Antiquarian*

Cover: Martinsell from the east;

Overleaf: Roman road on North Down aligned to Silbury Hill

EXPLORING HISTORIC WILTSHIRE

Volume 1: North

Six districts of north Wiltshire: their history, landscapes and artistic associations – which offer the best walking in the county

Ken Watts

EX LIBRIS PRESS

Published in 1997
Reprinted with revisions in 2001 by
EX LIBRIS PRESS
1 The Shambles
Bradford on Avon
Wiltshire BA15 1JS

Design and typesetting by
Ex Libris Press

Cover printed by
Shires Press, Trowbridge

Printed and bound by
Cromwell Press
Trowbridge, Wiltshire

ISBN 0 948578 85 8

*This book is dedicated to the late G. B. B.
who loved to walk in Wiltshire.*

Contents

About the Author

Ken Watts was born at Devizes in 1933 and has lived for most of his life in Wiltshire. His interest in local history and topography is long-standing, and since his retirement in 1989 from his profession as an architect he has devoted much of his time to these interests. Over the past thirty years he has become familiar with rural Wiltshire by regularly walking in the county and studying its history. For several years he was a Countryside Commission's part-time warden on the Wiltshire section of the Ridgeway, and he has led a great many guided walks in the Wiltshire countryside for many organisations.

In addition to writing this book he took the photographs and drew the maps and line drawings. He has also published *Snap: the History, Depopulation and Destruction of a Wiltshire Village* (1989), *Droving in Wiltshire: the Trade and its Routes* (1990), and *The Marlborough Downs* (1993), as well as magazine articles. He has undertaken detailed research – as yet unpublished – into medieval deer parks and the landscapes of Southern England associated with the life and writings of the poet Edward Thomas.

Author's Note

Throughout this book a number of prehistoric and historical periods are frequently referred to. These periods, with their approximate dates, are as follows:

Neolithic (or New Stone Age): BC 3500 to 2000.
Bronze Age: BC 2000 to 800.
Iron Age: BC 800 to AD 43.
Romano-British: AD 43 to 410.
Post-Roman: AD 410 to 500.
Anglo-Saxon: AD 500 to 1066.
Medieval: 1066 to 1485.
Tudor: 1485 to 1603.
Stuart: 1603 to 1714.
Georgian: 1714 to 1837.
Victorian: 1837 to 1901.

Introduction

This book is written for those who believe that one of the strongest aspects of the countryside is not visual but lies in the invisible history that lies concealed in the landscape. It is the culmination of many years spent by its author walking rural Wiltshire, researching its history, leading guided walks, and acquiring the knowledge which is now passed on to his readers. This is the first of two volumes devoted to exploring on foot the rural parts of Wiltshire. The present volume covers six extensive areas of North Wiltshire extending as far south and including the Vale of Pewsey. A companion volume *Exploring Historic Wiltshire Volume 2: South* describes six more areas south of Pewsey Vale.

The importance of the historical background was aptly expressed by Hilaire Belloc when he wrote in *The Old Road* (1904): 'By the recovery of the Past, stuff and being are added to us; our lives which, lived in the present only, are a film or surface, take on body – are lifted into one dimension more. The soul is fed', and in *The South Country* (1909) Edward Thomas, who was a connoisseur of the landscape of the south of England, wrote: 'There are many places that nobody can look upon without being consciously influenced by a sense of their history'.

This book describes the walking that is available in six of the finest districts of rural North Wiltshire. The topography of those areas and the way in which man has moulded the landscape is described, as is the visible prehistory and the history of the areas described, together with their literary associations, aspects which although not visible add a vital extra dimension the appreciation and enjoyment of landscape. Although its subjects have been researched in depth, this is essentially an outdoor book intended for those who wish to explore the rural parts of Wiltshire.

From long experience of leading innumerable guided walks over many years I have become aware that many walkers with a feeling for the past wish to know something of the history that lies behind the landscapes in which they walk. As for myself, when walking in an unfamiliar landscape I find myself irritated at my lack of knowledge of its historical background; that landscape lacks the vital extra dimension which a knowledge of its history would provide. The field antiquities are described as components in the landscape, and the history and literary associations are closely related to the countrysides described. This book is written both for local people who wish to extend their walking into new districts, and for those who do not yet know Wiltshire but are interested in exploring the county.

In *The Making of the English Landscape* (1955) Professor W.G. Hoskins demonstrated that the English landscape is a palimpsest upon which the history of England is visibly etched to be read by the informed observer. He suggests that one cannot understand the English landscape and enjoy it to the full 'without going back to the history that lies behind it'. Professor Hoskins also suggested that poets make the best topographers, and the poet Edward Thomas, who loved Wiltshire, noted in *The South Country* (1909) that 'the landscape retains the most permanent marks of the past'.

This book describes what Professor Hoskins called the 'observables' in the landscape. It is written for those who in their walking in North Wiltshire wish to know of the history that lies concealed behind the visible landscape of Wiltshire, a county which is particularly richly endowed with archaeological field monuments and historical associations. Each chapter takes as its subject a specific area which offers good walking, and provides a wide-ranging, in-depth study of the landscape and its asociations.

Many walkers recognise that almost as much pleasure is obtained from planning walks as from walking them. Consequently much scope is left for readers to use this book as a basis for devising their own walks to take in those landscape features which interest them, always following the public rights of way shown on the Landranger or Explorer Ordnance Survey maps. Nevertheless, for less experienced walkers, each chapter ends with a number of suggestions for walks in general terms. These suggestions are in no way comprehensive; the 'Suggested walks' sections simply describe routes of walks which the author has particularly enjoyed which readers may choose to follow.

Wiltshire is dominated by the Downs. About two-thirds of the county lies on the chalk and everyone who would know Wiltshire must know her Downs. For this reason the greater part of this book is devoted to the areas of chalk downland which are at the very heart of the county. Well known areas such as the Ridgeway are included, as are some less well known landscapes.

A desirable characteristic in any walking book is that it should be compact and portable. This book is consequently small in format. Some outline maps are included, but it is emphasised that these are merely sketch maps included to indicate the locations of places mentioned in the text. They contain insufficient detail to be regarded as walking maps and are no substitute for the Ordnance Survey maps which, with their definitive indication of all public rights of way, are essential for all walkers in England. Two sheets of the 1: 50,000 Landrangers maps (numbered 173 and 174) cover most of North Wiltshire (numbers 183 and 184 cover most of South Wiltshire). The numbers of the relevant Landranger maps are given at the head of each chapter. The larger scale Explorer maps are an alternative to the Landrangers.

In order to avoid the necessity for long descriptions of location in rural areas where landmarks are few, six-figure map references are sometimes used in brackets in the text – for example (149763). These refer to the National Grid and relate to the Ordnance Survey maps. The prefixes ST and SU relevant to Wiltshire have been omitted from all map references in the interests of brevity. An explanation of the easily mastered National Grid reference system is given on all Ordnance Survey maps.

It remains to me to make some acknowledgements, first to the staff of Wiltshire Local Studies Library and Wiltshire Record Office for unfailing assistance. Then to my friend Michael Higham with whom I have walked more miles than with any other person over the past thirty years, and to all the people – many of them unknown to me by name on guided walks – with whom I have walked and talked when acquiring the knowledge that has gone into this book. I also acknowledge my indebtedness to the writings of the late Professor W.G. Hoskins and the theories on the evolution of the landscape which he first propounded in *The Making of the English Landscape* (1955):

> The English landscape itself, to those who know how to read it aright, is the richest historical record we possess. There are discoveries to be made in it for which no written documents exist, or have ever existed. There is no part of England, however unpromising it may appear at first sight, that is not full of questions for those who have a sense of the past.

Ken Watts
Trowbridge, Wiltshire
March 2001

N
Malmesbury
Swindon
Malmesbury
Plain
Ridgeway
4: GRIGSON COUNTRY
1: RIDGEWAY COUNTRY
2: THE CENTRAL MARLBOROUGHDOWNS
5: CALSTONE, OLDBURY & ROUNDWAY DOWN
Marlborough
3: WANSDYKE
6: THE VALE OF PEWSEY
Devizes
Pewsey
Trowbridge
Salisbury
7: CHUTE CAUSEWAY
Plain
Warminster
R. Wylye
8: THE WYLYE VALLEY
9: WILTSHIRE SELWOOD & WHITE SHEET DOWNS
10: GREAT RIDGE WOOD & GROVELY WOOD
Salisbury
The Salisbury Way
11: THE SOUTH WILTSHIRE RIDGEWAYS
Ox Drove
12: SOUTH-EAST WILTSHIRE
0 5 10 15 Kilometres
0 5 10 Miles

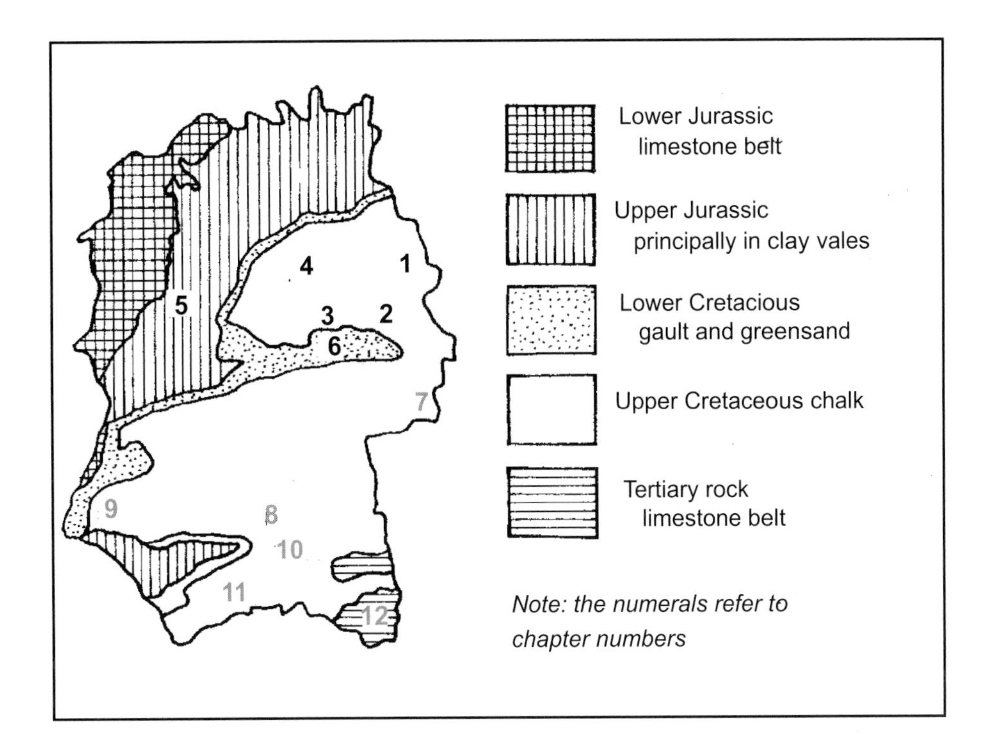

Above: Geological Map of Wiltshire

Opposite: Map of Wiltshire indicating the 12 districts featured in Exploring Historic Wiltshire, Volume 1: North Wiltshire *(1 to 6)*
Volume 2: South Wiltshire *features the second six (7 to 12)*

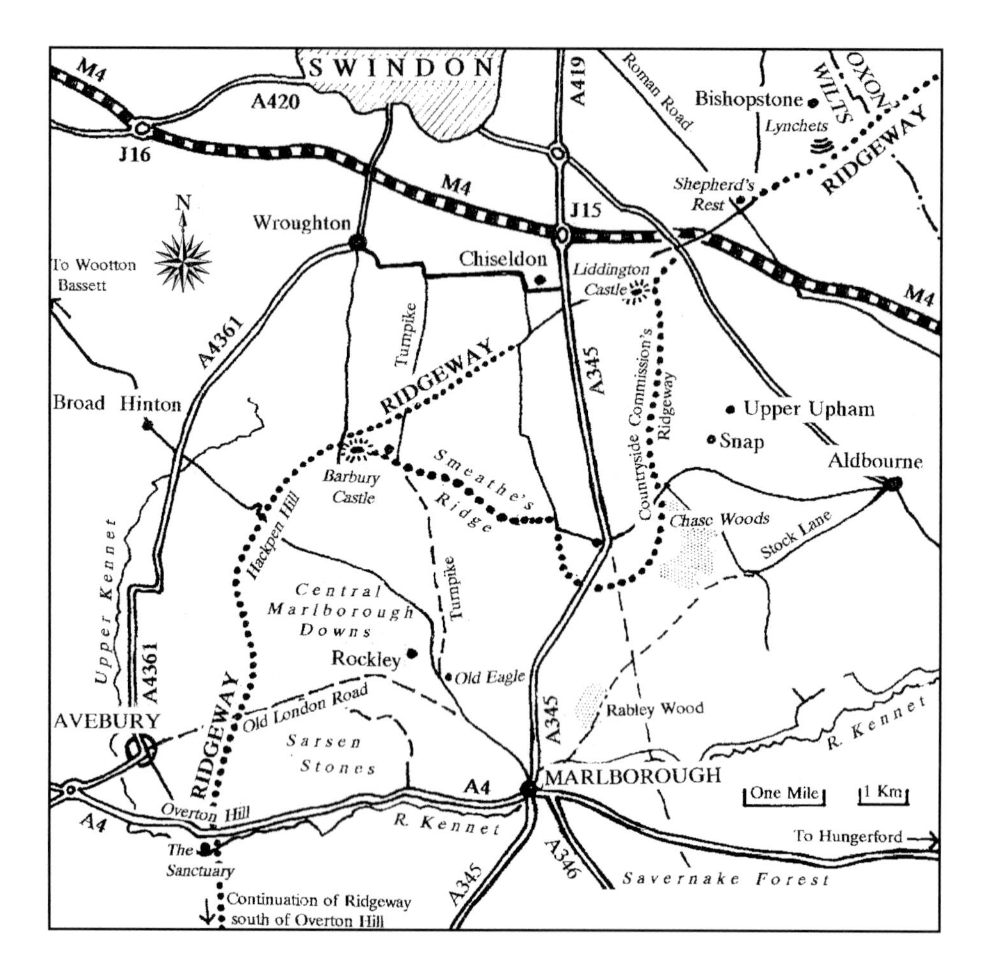

Ridgeway Country

1 Ridgeway Country

Bishopstone, Liddington, Snap and Upham, Barbury and Hackpen Hill

(maps Landranger 173 and 174)

The best-known walking in Wiltshire is provided by the Ridgeway which attracts many long-distance walkers to the county. It enters Wiltshire from Oxfordshire – formerly Berkshire – above the village of Bishopstone in the extreme north-east of Wiltshire, and crosses the Marlborough Downs in its progression westwards from its crossing of the Thames at Streatley to near Avebury, and beyond.

The Ridgeway is an ancient hilltop trackway which has been called 'the oldest road'. This old way from Norfolk to Wiltshire, and perhaps beyond Wiltshire to the Dorset coast, was known as the Icknield Way, but after its crossing of the Thames it split into two. The track now called the Ridgeway follows the high and dry ground across the downs. The other track, which runs as a parallel way along the foot of the downs, retains the name Icknield Way.

The incidence of prehistoric monuments along its route suggests that the Ridgeway was in use in prehistoric times. Many Romano-British sites occur beside it, and it was certainly used in early historic times when, during the Anglo-Saxon colonisation of Britain and the subsequent Viking invasions, several battles were fought beside the Ridgeway which then served as a convenient long distance route for warring armies. It continued to be used by travellers, traders and drovers until the development, in the 17th and 18th centuries, of a convenient system of roads over lower ground and the coming of the railways in the 19th century took away most of its traffic. Having been an ancient communication route the Ridgeway remains today a public right of way. It provides admirable upland recreational facilities for walkers and riders, and it has been designated by the Countryside Commission an official Long Distance Trail administered through the Ridgeway Officer at Oxford.

Unfortunately over much of its length the Ridgeway has also been officially designated a 'byway' – that is technically a route open to all traffic. It is consequently frequently used by motorised traffic which is encouraged by the policy of its guardians the Countryside Commission of laying stone surfacing along the ancient green way, erecting signs, and utterly destroying the character of the Ridgeway which has been admired by informed opinion over a great many years. This unfortunate policy is alleged to be for the convenience of all users, but it in my estimation – and I served for some years as a Ridgeway Warden on the Wiltshire section of the Ridgeway – merely encourages more motor vehicles to use the Ridgeway.

Having run for many miles from its crossing of the Thames at Streatley in a westerly direction, south of Uffington White Horse the Ridgeway swings gently south-west and, after passing Wayland's Smithy long barrow, enters Wiltshire (at 259833) a little east of Bishopstone. After half a mile the way crosses a metalled track at Ridgeway Farm, one of the few buildings situated beside the Ridgeway in Wiltshire. This cross-track runs on south to serve a former Romano-British site (259816) on Russley Downs.

Ridgeway descending Fox Hill with Liddington Clump (left) ahead.

Bishopstone and its Lynchets

A particularly beautiful but little known area of Wiltshire lies around Bishopstone immediately north of the Ridgeway. Here may be seen a fine downland village associated with one of the most delightful coombes in English downland, a coombe which at some undetermined date has been modelled by the creation of a magnificent series of strip-lynchets along its sides and across its head equal to any in the English countryside.

Bishopstone village is a place of great antiquity and considerable beauty. It is associated with the two very ancient ways which have already been mentioned, the Icknield Way and the Ridgeway. The village stands on the Icknield Way (now the B4507 road) about a mile north of the Ridgeway.

Two villages with the name of Bishopstone exist today in Wiltshire. One is the fine village in south Wiltshire situated in the valley of the River Ebble and about five miles south-west of Salisbury. It is also said that the name of Bushton near Wootton Bassett is a corruption of Bishopstone. The Bishopstone associated with the Ridgeway is a downland village located towards the west end of the Vale of White Horse about six miles east of Swindon.

The general lack of awareness of Bishopstone east of Swindon is probably due to its situation at the very extremity of north-east Wiltshire near the county boundary between Wiltshire and Oxfordshire, a situation which leads to uncertainty about whether the Bishopstone area truly belongs to the Marlborough Downs or to the Vale of White Horse, for in some ways it belongs more to the latter than to the Wiltshire Downs. The name Bishopstone means 'Bishop's farm or estate', the parish having formerly been part of Ramsbury which was a possession of the Bishops of Salisbury.

The Wiltshire writer Alfred Williams (1877-1930) rated Bishopstone, in *Villages of the White Horse* (1913), 'the prettiest of all the down-side, taken all round'. He described the large squarish mill-pool at the centre of the village with the mill opposite which has now been converted into a dwelling, and emphasised the way in which the elm trees of Bishopstone embowered the village on three sides. These elms have now disappeared having inevitably fallen victims to Dutch elm disease.

In common with the other villages of north-west Wiltshire, Bishopstone is constructed of a variety of building materials including chalk block – known locally as 'clunch' – flint, and brick. Some cottage walls are of clunch laced with brick string-courses and are strengthened by brick quoins. Others consist of a varied but harmonious amalgam of materials, generally with brick chimneys. The roofs are usually of thatch, but there is some tile. This almost invariable use of traditional indigenous materials led H.W. Timperley to suggest in *Ridge Way Country* that the village 'snuggled into the downs as if it had grown there rather than been built'. Many of the garden walls are of clunch blocks with a capping of overhanging thatch and footings of sarsen stone, the two providing the 'good hat and boots' which is necessary to preserve the vulnerable clunch masonry which is liable to disintegrate if not protected from the ravages of the weather and rising damp.

The prominent towered church of St Mary, which stands in the lower part of Bishopstone to the north of the Icknield Way, incorporates re-used Norman features in a predominantly Perpendicular rebuilding.

Bishopstone Coombe from near the Ridgeway

The great glory of Bishopstone is its coombe with its magnificent series of strip-lynchets, which runs from the village towards the downs and the Ridgeway. When the poet Edward Thomas came this way in 1911 he drew particular attention in his book *The Icknield Way* to these strip-lynchets which exist on both the shoulders and across the head of the wide flat-bottomed coombe which winds southwards from the village and forks as it runs up into the downs. In *The Oldest Road: An Exploration of the Ridgeway*, J.R.L. Anderson described the Bishopstone lynchets as being 'though on a smaller scale, as perfect as anything to be seen on a Mediterranean hillside, where peasant industry over the centuries has terraced steep surfaces for vines or olive groves'.

Strip-lynchets are perhaps the most misunderstood of archaeological field monuments. They occur frequently in the chalk downlands of southern England, a fact noted by William Cobbett (1763-1835) when he wrote in his *Rural Rides* of the 'hundreds of acres of ploughed land in shelves' which he had seen on his travels. They were formed over many years as heavy ploughing of the slopes led to a gradual displacement of topsoil down the slope. This topsoil accumulated at intervals to create the horizontal terraces described by Cobbett as 'shelves'.

Many theories have been advanced to explain strip-lynchets, but the consensus of opinion suggests that they are merely the natural consequence of extending agriculture up steep hillsides and were not deliberately constructed, although when they are as substantial as these examples at Bishopstone it seems probable that they originated as the natural result of ploughsoil drifting downhill and were then deliberately enlarged as the villagers widened the flat treads of the terraces to extend the area available for cultivation. The flat areas (or treads) were cultivated, and the steeply sloping faces of the steps (or risers), being too steep to plough, remained uncultivated. The contrast in texture between the rank grass of the risers and the now-grazed flat surfaces of the terraces accentuates the character of strip-lynchets. Sometimes ramps were provided up the lynchets to provide access. Strip-lynchets generally follow the contours in the form of a series of giant steps, a fact which has led them to become popularly known as 'shepherds' steps'.

The dates of origin of strip-lynchets are difficult to establish and the subject is a matter of some debate. They are often assumed to be prehistoric, although they are more likely to be medieval. H.J. Massingham believed them to be Anglo-Saxon when he wrote in *English Downland*: 'The finest of these Saxon strips, lynchetts or terraces, survive above Bishopstone.' It is entirely possible that strip-lynchets existed in the Romano-British period, although it is more probable that the earliest examples are Anglo-Saxon. The Belgic people who preceded the Romans in the last phase of the Iron Age introduced the heavy plough which had the capacity to make strip-lynchets, but there is no definite evidence of strip-lynchets originating in the Belgic or Romano-British periods and whenever they occur in association with Belgic or Roman sites they have invariably been demonstrated to be medieval in origin.

It is arguable that, because of the immense effort necessary to construct them and the difficulties experienced when ploughing on the hillsides which they occupy, strip-lynchets reflect the land-hunger of a rapidly expanding population. This makes them likely to have been constructed in the 12th or 13th century or a little earlier, at the time when the population was increasing prior to the arrival of the Black Death which depleted the population by a third to a half in the second half of the 14th century. Once they had been created, strip-lynchets sometimes continued to be cultivated until comparatively recent times, for example at Calstone Wellington near Calne where they were cultivated well into the 18th century.

Bishopstone lynchets from the west

The strip-lynchets at Bishopstone face north and are sheltered by the downs to their south from the prevailing winds. It is possibly significant that they are not visible from the Ridgeway which runs along the downs a little to their north, and are not readily seen from the Icknield Way as it runs through the village. This may represent a deliberate attempt by the villagers in lawless times to conceal their agricultural activities and crops from marauders passing along these two ancient routes. The lynchets consist of seven horizontal terraces and eight angled risers, the treads averaging about 40 feet (12m) wide and the risers about 10 to 13 feet (3 to 4m) high. Excavation of the Bishopstone lynchets in June 1955 (reported in *Wiltshire Archaeological Magazines* 56 and 57) failed to establish the date when they originated, but suggested that they continued to be cultivated until comparatively recent times. Today they are no longer used for arable crops and are now used as grazing for sheep and cattle.

At the bottom of the coombe, towards the village, the springs which formerly fed a thriving watercress industry issue from the spring line on the east flank of the coombe and feed the large pond at the centre of the village. Above this point the coombe is dry. The word 'coombe' (or 'combe') means valley, being related to the Welsh *cwm*, and in Wiltshire is usually applied to a riverless upland valley. On the east flank of the coombe stood the grove of trees marked on the maps as Bishopstone Folly (247831), now sadly reduced to a pair of sickly looking trees. The name 'folly' was often applied to clumps of trees planted for visual as opposed to utilitarian reasons, such aesthetic considerations being incomprehensible to many people and regarded as folly.

Down the east side of the coombe runs a belt of beech trees which, despite being very restricted in size due to their exposed situation, were mentioned by Timperley in 1935. Both shoulders of this coombe are terraced with single or double lynchets, although the principal Bishopstone lynchets – marked 'Field Systems' on the large scale maps – cross the head of the coombe a little to the north of the Ridgeway (244825). They are best appreciated when seen from the track which descends (242825) from the Ridgeway to Bishopstone village past the west end of the lynchets.

The Ridgeway

Returning to the Ridgeway, after crossing Charlbury Hill at a height of 782 feet (238m) the way descends the long descent of Totterdown with views of Liddington Clump and Barbury Castle ahead and crosses the Roman Ermin Way (now the road from Swindon to Baydon and Aldbourne) at Fox Hill (232813). Totterdown is an old name for a 'look-out place'. At the foot of the hill is The Shepherd's Rest Inn, formerly a cottage beer-house used by drovers taking their flocks and herds along the Ridgeway but now rebuilt as a prosperous inn. Westwards from The Shepherd's Rest the Ridgeway has been taken into the modern road system and becomes a metalled road as it crosses the M4 motorway by a road bridge on Wanborough Plain slightly south of its original line. At the crossing of the B4192 (formerly A419) Swindon to Aldbourne road there comes a parting of the ways.

The original ancient Ridgeway ran on south-west along the line of the present macadam road north of Liddington Hill and across the low-lying ground at the head of the Og Valley south of Chiseldon. It passed betwen Burderop Hackpen and Draycot Foliat and through the site of the former 19th century Burderop Racecourse at Mudgell (now 'Midge Hall' on the maps), described by Richard Jefferies in *World's End*, to pass north of Barbury Castle Iron Age hillfort and climb on to the north end of Hackpen Hill over Uffcott Down.

This old direct and now partly macadamed route of the Ridgeway across Wanborough Plain makes dull walking and, in order to avoid this low-lying and metalled stretch between Liddington Hill and Barbury, the Countryside Commission has adopted a diversionary high level route for its Long Distance Trail, looping south over Round Hill Downs and crossing the Og Valley at Southend. At the crossing of the Swindon to Aldbourne road (B4192) the Countryside Commission's Ridgeway follows the B4192 south-east for about a hundred yards and then (at 218804) follows a long gentle climb south-westwards to pass south of Liddington Iron Age hillfort at a height of about 900 feet (274m). It then swings south to gently descend the ridge along Whitefield Hill. This Countryside Commission diversion from the Ridgeway may always have been an alternative Ridgeway route as it follows more high ground than the direct route from Liddington Hill to Barbury Castle, plunging only to cross the head of the River Og at Southend.

Liddington Hill

A case can be made, largely on the basis of its proximity to Badbury and its former name of Badbury Camp, for Liddington Hill having been the site of the decisive late-5th or early-6th century Battle of Badon (*Mons Badonicus*) at which the Britons under Arthur severely checked the advance of the Saxons into Wiltshire. Liddington Hill will be forever associated with the country writer Richard Jefferies (1848-1887) who in his youth used to walk there from his home at Coate near Swindon and sit at the south-west corner of the hillfort at the point (207796) where the ramparts have slipped. From here he could look south-west over the valley of the Og and think the thoughts that he later expressed in his spiritual biography *The Story of My Heart*. Although there are no designated public footpaths on to Liddington, the hillfort may be visited by following the 'permissive path', opened by arrangement with the landowner, which is signed as it runs north and west along field edges from the Ridgeway path (at 213797).

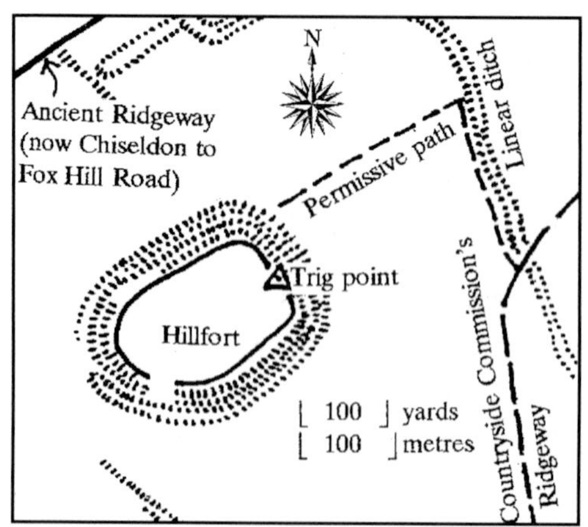

On the continuation of the Ridgeway over its gentle descent southwards from Liddington Hill fine views are seen west over the Og Valley and to the east along Shipley Bottom to Sugar Hill and over Aldbourne. On Whitefield Hill the Ridgeway passes between Lower Upham and Upper Upham. This way running south from Liddington used to be followed by the poet Charles Sorley (1895-1915), who became a victim of the Great War, on his way back to Marlborough School. His love of the Marlborough Downs was so great that he would leave his train at a remote station in the Berkshire Downs in order to walk back to Marlborough through the Berkshire Vale of the White Horse and along the Ridgeway past Liddington Hill, turning south along this way to Marlborough.

In addition to being intrinsically beautiful – it was described by Edward Thomas as 'a beautiful, a quiet, an unrenowned, and a most visibly ancient land' – the fine area of broken countryside between Marlborough and Swindon at the north edge of Aldbourne Chase is a delightfully secluded area which provides some of the best walking in the North Wiltshire Downs. A rich historic back-ground always gives an added dimension to the enjoyment of landscape and this area has many historical associations extending from prehistoric to recent times. The area of which I write is that bounded to the west by the A345 former Roman road along the Og Valley, to its east by the B4192 road, by Liddington Hill to the north, and Aldbourne Chase to its south. The Ridgeway Long Distance recreational way follows the western edge of the area which is also crossed by many other public rights-of-way which provide excellent access and an infinite variety of walks.

This countryside south and west of the Ridgeway contains an abundance of prehistoric remains including early field systems and tumuli, the burial mounds of the Bronze Age. Some of these are scattered on either side of the B4192, and others delineate the ancient trackway which runs south-east from Upper Upham towards Aldbourne. One of the tumuli beside this way has acquired the name of The Giant's Grave (246764), but the the most dramatically sited are the Four Barrows on the crest of Sugar Hill which lie strictly outside my area but are very visible from it.

A Roman road follows the pass of the River Og parallel to the Ridgeway and a little to its west. Richard Jefferies recorded seeing a Roman tesselated floor on the ridge overlooking this road above Lower Upham, and the Romans were also present on the ridge at Upper Upham which provides a rare example of an upland site continuously occupied from prehistoric to modern times. The twin Iron Age earthwork hillforts of Barbury and Liddington 'Castles' at its northern end emphasise the strategic importance of the Og Valley as a direct pass into Wiltshire from the north which saw great activity when the Saxons were expanding into Wiltshire from the Thames Valley in their take-over of Wessex after the departure of the Romans.

Richard Jefferies and Edward Thomas

This entire area of 'Ridgeway Country' at the northern edge of the Marlborough Downs is inevitably associated with the local writer and historian Richard Jefferies. Here Jefferies wandered and mused, and pondered the thoughts that ultimately led him to refuse to follow his father into small-scale farming at Coate Farm and become a writer. In his early days as a local journalist Jefferies wrote many local history articles on North Wiltshire which were gathered into a book called *Jefferies' Land* (1896) by its editor Grace Toplis. Long after he had left Wiltshire to spend his last ten years nearer his publishers in London and remote from his native county, most of the experiences which went into his writings were obtained during his early years of wandering in these Marlborough Downs.

At about the time that Richard Jefferies died in exile from his beloved Wiltshire, his biographer the walker-poet Edward Thomas (1878-1917) discovered Wiltshire on schoolboy holidays with his grandmother at Swindon. Thomas emulated Jefferies by spending many boyhood days wandering the Marlborough Down countryside around Swindon. After establishing some reputation as a critic and writer of beautiful prose, Thomas suddenly launched into poetry and during the last two years of his life wrote the verse for which he is now justly famous.

The Wiltshire Downs south of Swindon were the first real countryside that he experienced, for he was born in London to Welsh parents. On many boyhood visits to Swindon in the 1880s and 1890s he became familiar with Burderop, Liddington and Barbury Castles, and as an adult Thomas regularly continued to visit this part of Wiltshire. The introductory chapter ('The Country of Richard Jefferies') to Edward Thomas's biography of Jefferies still provides an excellent introduction to the landscapes of this district although, unlike Jefferies whose Wiltshire writings were restricted to the north-east of the county, the walking of Edward Thomas in Wiltshire was not restricted to the Marlborough Downs. He grew to know the whole of rural Wiltshire intimately and regarded Wiltshire as his spiritual home. Having taken a history degree at Oxford, Thomas often pretended a disregard for the history of the countryside, but he was in fact profoundly influenced by the history of his 'South Country' which recurs throughout his writings.

Opposite: Edward Thomas (left) and Richard Jefferies (right)

Upper Upham and Snap

Deserted villages are generally subjects of interest, and this area has two deserted villages in Upper Upham and Snap which both appeared – as *Upham* and *Snappe* – in the 1332 Wiltshire Tax Lists. There is as much contrast in the history of these two villages as there is in their siting. Upper Upham is on the crown a high hill and its present buildings are, with the exception of the manor house, all modern. Henry III in 1229 gave Aldbourne Manor, which included Upper Upham and Snap, to his half-brother William Longespée, the fourth Earl of Salisbury, and he in turn donated Upper Upham to Lacock Abbey. In 1365 Aldbourne Manor came into the possession of John of Gaunt when the manors of Aldbourne and Trowbridge were settled on him.

John of Gaunt (1340-1399) – Shakespeare's 'time-honoured Lancaster' – was the third son of Edward III and the father of Henry IV (1367-1413). He became Duke of Lancaster in 1362 as a result of his marriage to Blanche, heiress to the Duchy. Blanche died in 1369, and John of Gaunt then married Constance, daughter of Pedro of Castile, and in 1372 assumed the title of King of Castile by right of his wife. His acquisitions at Aldbourne included Upper Upham and Aldbourne Chase, a 'chase' being a hunting ground similar to a royal forest but owned by a subject. John of Gaunt owned manors all over England and is said to have owned a third of the country. He effectively owned a state within a state but must often have been at Aldbourne for the good hunting in Aldbourne Chase, and he is believed to have had a hunting lodge at Upper Upham. There is a local tradition that Upham situated on its hill, lacked a water supply and that John of Gaunt had to go down to Aldbourne village for his baths. His hunting lodge was probably at or near

Above: Upper Upham Manor House
Below: Snap and Upham

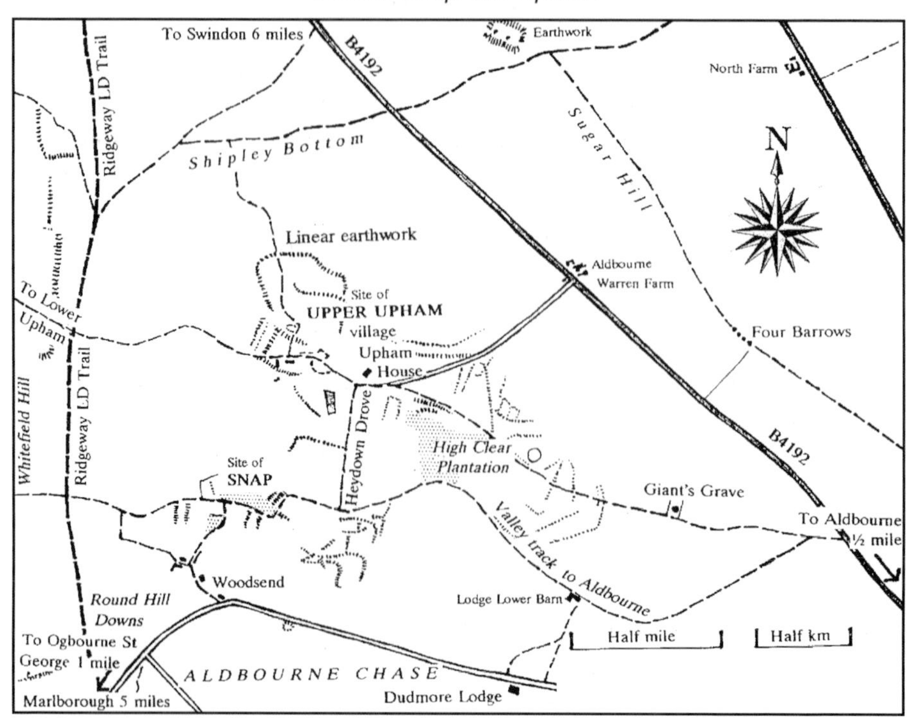

the site of the present Upper Upham Manor House.

During the minority (1377-1386) of his nephew Richard of Bordeaux (Richard II), John of Gaunt was effectively ruler of England. He was immensely powerful and ambitious, and was believed to be intriguing against his nephew and to have aspirations to the throne of England. He was blamed for many of the ills of the time, and one of the principal demands of the peasants during the Peasants' Revolt in 1381 was the head of John of Gaunt on a pike, but he was away campaigning in Scotland and the rebels had to content themselves with sacking his palace at The Savoy on The Strand. When his second wife Constance died in 1394 Gaunt married his mistress Catherine Swynford. Their children were legitimised in 1397 as the Beauforts.

John of Gaunt died in 1399. He never became king, but at his death Richard II took the opportunity of eliminating the impossible anachronism of a state within a state by confiscating all the estates of John of Gaunt's son Henry Bolingbroke, Earl of Derby and Hereford. Henry Bolingbroke had shown disloyalty to King Richard and was in exile for brawling at Court. Richard extended his exile from ten years to life but this precipitate attempt to solve the problem which the vast Duchy of Lancaster posed to the Crown was to be Richard's downfall for it provoked Henry Bolingbroke, now also Duke of Lancaster, to in 1400 return, usurp the throne as Henry IV, and finally resolve the problem by taking the Duchy of Lancaster estates to the Crown.

Geoffrey Chaucer (c1340-1400) was in John of Gaunt's service. He came from humble origins but was brought up as a page at the court of Edward III. In about 1367 Chaucer married Philippe de Rouet who was a lady-in-waiting to the queen and a sister of Catherine Swynford, John of Gaunt's mistress and ultimate third wife. Three years after John of Gaunt acquired Aldbourne Manor Chaucer produced his first major poem 'The Death of Blanche the Duchess', an allegory upon the death of John of Gaunt's first wife from the plague in 1369.

Chaucer died in 1400, the year following the death of John of Gaunt. Having been in his service Chaucer would almost certainly have known Upper Upham and may have hunted there. When walking down the long slope from Upper Upham towards Aldbourne I invariably imagine John of Gaunt and his entourage, including his son who was to become king as Henry IV and Geoffrey Chaucer, following this way down to the village after hunting to take their baths at Aldbourne.

At the Dissolution of the Monasteries, Upper Upham was sold in 1539 to the Abbess of Lacock's tenant John Goddard, 'woolman', then a grazier at Upham. The acquisition of the fine property at Upham consolidated the fortunes of this great landowning family of north Wiltshire, and it was probably John Goddard's son Thomas who rebuilt the the manor house in the late 16th century. After the Goddards removed to Swindon, Upper Upham Manor House fell into dereliction and was in the mid-19th century occupied by a labourer known to Richard Jefferies. When he was researching his biography of Richard Jefferies in 1908 Edward Thomas discovered the derelict manor and described the house:

> One of the noblest views of the downs and the northern country towards the Cotswolds and Malvern Hills is to be had from the roof of the Elizabethan manor-house at Upper Upham; the legend is that Wales, too, can be seen. This handsome, remote house, high on the hills, reputed to be on the site of a hunting-lodge of John of Gaunt, was described at length by Jefferies as a young man and archaeologist. He knew the tenant. It is empty now.
>
> (from *Richard Jefferies*, 1909)

In its derelict condition the manor house was purchased in about 1910 by Miss Hanham (1872-1939) who discovered it on a sketching tour. When she married Sir James Currie in 1913 they sensitively rebuilt and extended the house using Biddulph Pinchard as their architect, not Edwin Lutyens as has sometimes been suggested. The front of the old house was taken down and re-assembled as the centrepiece of a largely new house. Today, Upper Upham Manor is divided into several dwellings.

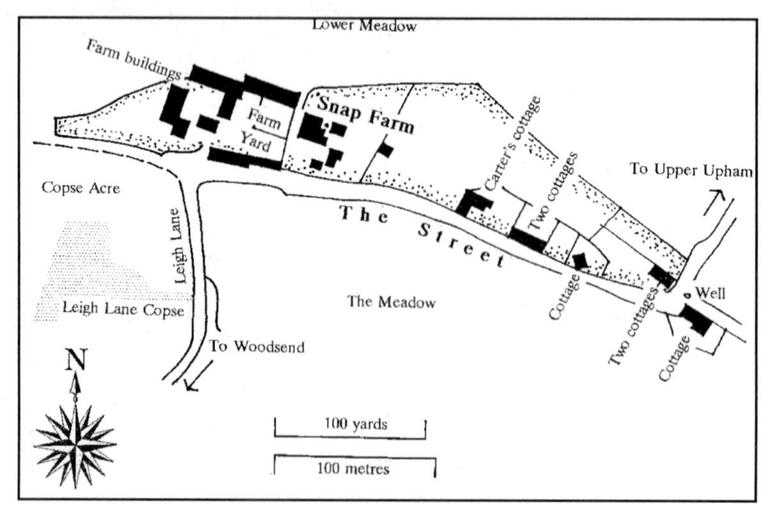

Plan of Snap in 1900, a little before it was finally abandoned.

Snap in its secluded coombe bottom below Upper Upham has a very different history. It is an example which is unique in Wiltshire and rare in the whole of England of a village depopulated and ultimately destroyed as recently as the present century, a victim of Victorian agricultural depression. Having survived for centuries in its remote downland coombe utterly dependent upon Snap Farm for employment, Snap ultimately fell victim to the depression that resulted from the importation in the 1870s of vast amounts of corn as the prairies of the American West were opened up. For a time the village struggled on but gradually the younger people drifted away to seek employment elsewhere and only two old couples in their eighties were left at Snap. Both of the Smiths died, as did James Fisher, leaving old Rachel Fisher as the last resident of Snap in about 1905. As the cottages fell empty the land was acquired by a local butcher-grazier called Henry Wilson who has been unfairly blamed for depopulating the already vacated village.

All the buildings at Snap are now demolished, and the village site in its wooded hollow in the downs exhibits that peculiar air of melancholy sometimes felt in places that have been inhabited for hundreds of years but are now deserted and desolate. These feelings are particularly poignant when the site of Snap is visited alone, perhaps because, unlike the many medieval depopulations, this village survived into modern times and the names of its residents and the sites of the houses which they occupied are known.

The former Snap village street, looking east

The Civil War engagement in Aldbourne Chase

A great event occurred in this district during the Civil War when in September 1643 Parliament's Lord General Essex led his army consisting of ten thousand foot, which included the London Trained Bands, four thousand cavalry and a number of field guns, across this area after his masterly success in raising the royalist seige of Gloucester. He was attempting to sneak his large army along the valley east of Snap past the site of Lodge Lower Barn (240759) – which did not then exist – on his return to London. The valley road from Snap to Aldbourne north of Dudmore Lodge is directly on the line of march to be expected by an army marching from Chiseldon to Aldbourne, and it is just such a road as one would expect a general to choose when wishing to avoid action and move a large force near an opposing army. From Cirencester through Cricklade to Swindon, Essex had followed Roman roads, but from Chiseldon he would probably have climbed over the shoulder of Liddington Hill by the little road past Folly Farm – 'Folly Barn' on Andrews and Dury – for the climb up the escarpment at Lower Upham would have been very steep for gun-hauling. He would then probably have continued through Upper Upham or Snap to the valley where the action took place. He was most likely discovered as his long column covered the open ground over the shoulder of Liddington Hill.

The engagement in Aldbourne Chase has been dismissed as a mere skirmish by some historians, although Clarendon – the Royalist historian of the war – described it as 'very sharp for an hour or two'. It should be appreciated that Parliament's ten thousand infantry marching three abreast in column of route –then called the 'long march' – would have extended over about four miles, from Aldbourne back along the valley past Lodge Lower Barn, up the Heydown Drove and west of Upper Upham to the Ridgeway crossing above Lower Upham Farm. The four thousand cavalry would, particularly after Prince Rupert made contact, have been thrown out to screen the infantry from charges by the 'near four thousand' (Clarendon) Royalist cavalry. Colonel Hurry, the scoutmaster who had discovered Essex on the march, harried the rear of the column with a thousand horse, while Prince Rupert with the remaining three thousand attacked the flank and 'routed them with good execution' (Clarendon).

That a running engagement continued along the valley is suggested by the bodies found when the egg-packing station was built west of Aldbourne, by the fact that overturned ammunition waggons were blown up in Aldbourne, and by the corpses of sixty men found shallowly buried during road-building in 1815 at Preston, a little south-east of Aldbourne. These were reburied in Aldbourne churchyard.

The valley running east from Snap to Aldbourne. Down this slope Prince Rupert's Royalist cavalry attacked the Parliamentarian army marching along the valley.

The unnamed valley under Dudmore Lodge has changed very little since 1643. Standing beside Lodge Lower Barn, the scene as the Parliamentary army was attacked by Prince Rupert's massed cavalry is easily imagined. If they had left Chiseldon at 6.00a.m. and, hindered by their guns, had maintained a pace of one and a half miles an hour, they would have been below Dudmore Lodge at about 10 to 11 o'clock. The horse teams dragging the guns would be being urged to increase the pace as they struggled through the valley bottom mud, for we know that the weather was very wet. The screening cavalry would be on the down along the flanks, for they would have realised that they had been sighted by Colonel Hurry's patrol which may have been keeping pace with them along the ridge. Then the feverish activity as the main body of Royalist cavalry appeared in great numbers and began to form up around Dudmore Lodge for the charge, the shouted orders to form circles – not squares in those days – by the infantry, and the unhitching and manhandling of their 'drake' field guns into firing position.

The uphill attack by the Parliamentary cavalry upon the Royalist horse before they could properly form up was described by Sergeant Foote of the Trained Bands: 'Col. Hervice's troops drew up in a body and gave the enemy a very fierce charge, which was performed with as brave a courage as men ever did'. Then the discharge of the guns into the Royalist cavalry massing around Dudmore, which may have led the Ordnance Survey – from the discovery there of round shot – to place their crossed swords indicating the site of the battle on their early large scale maps on the ridge, followed by the downhill charge of Rupert's cavalry in the new 'Swedish drill' of three widely spaced ranks which Rupert had learned during his service with Gustave Adolphus of Sweden, rather than the old-fashioned method of six closely spaced ranks. This would have been followed by close quarter fighting as the Royalist cavalry with sabre and pistol tried to break the 'hedges' of pikes and get among the musketeers who were pouring their fire into the Royalist horse. That they succeeded in breaking at least some of the defensive rings is suggested by Clarendon's statement that they 'routed them with good execution'.

Two months earlier, at the Battle of Roundway Down (see Chapter 5) the Royalist cavalry under Lord Wilmot, who commanded one of the cavalry brigades here in Aldbourne Chase, had unsupported by infantry or artillery routed a superior balanced army of infantry, cavalry, and artillery, commanded by the redoubtable Sir William Waller who had been so successful early in the Civil War that he became known as William the Conqueror.

In passing it should be noted that Aldbourne Manor had in 1624 been settled on the king, when he was Prince Charles. As king, in 1626 Charles sold the manor to the City of London, but had retained The Chase and The Warren. It was a strange quirk of fate that King Charles's army found itself engaging in Aldbourne Chase the City of London trained bands at the very turning point of the war, for there is little doubt that had Parliament's London Army been brought to action and defeated during its return march to London the war would have been decided in the king's favour. But King Charles failed to bring the Royalist infantry up, Essex ultimately succeeded in returning to London with the last Parliamentary field army left in southern England, and the chance of a possibly decisive victory for the king in the Civil War was lost.

Aldbourne's countryside

During early medieval times Aldbourne Chase was reserved for the hunting of deer at large and wild deer are today often seen in the area. Later these uplands were used to graze sheep and rabbits. Old farming traditions die hard here. Ploughing with ox teams continued well into the present century, and today in early spring old relics of a former sheep-rearing practice may be seen when mobile shepherd's huts are sometimes seen wheeled out into the lambing pens from Aldbourne Warren Farm. These huts were once a common sight in downland areas when the shepherd lived out in them for several weeks when the ewes requires frequent attention at lambing time. The shepherd's huts that are seen today are generally derelict or adapted to alternative uses. After first appearing in about 1840 they became very popular and were manufactured by most agricultural implements makers. The shepherd's hut consisted of a timber framed hut clad with corrugated iron and measuring about six feet by eight feet (1.8m by 2.4m) mounted on a timber undercarriage with cast iron wheels. There was a door at the rear end, generally of the 'stable' two-leaf type, reached by detachable steps, and a small window for ventilation. The shepherd's hut contained a bunk-bed and a cast iron stove for heating with a stove pipe run through the segmental roof. Although most examples seen today are derelict, they sometimes still bear their manufacturer's plate above the door at their rear end. In spring they were hauled out to the lambing pens by the towing-frame which was generally A-shaped and was hinged to fold back against the front wall of the hut. A derelict example of such a hut may be seen beside the Ridgeway (213794) a little south of Liddington Hill.

The former rabbit warrens are commemorated in the names of Liddington Warren Farm and Aldbourne Warren Farm beside the B4192. Another farming relic exists at Lower Upham Farm where a large timber 14 foot (4.26m) diameter treadwheel formerly operated by a donkey to raise water from a deep well is housed in an outbuilding. A similar donkey wheel once existed at Snap.

On his Rural Ride of 2 October 1826 William Cobbett wrote this rather contradictory appreciation of the countryside around Aldbourne:

> Along here, the country is rather too bare; here, until you come to Auburn, or Aldbourne, there are no meadows in the valleys, and no trees, even round the homesteads. This, therefore, is too naked to please me: but I love the downs so much, that, if I had to choose, I would live even here, and especially I would farm here.

The composer Gerald Finzi (1901-1956), who drew from the English landscape the inspiration for the gravely lyrical and very English music for which he is now gaining a belated reputation, lived for a time (1935-37) at the house called Beech Knoll on the north side of Aldbourne, and would have known the countryside around Snap and Upham.

One of the great delights of this area is Shipley Bottom (225784), the wide shallow coombe which runs eastwards from the Ridgeway south of

Liddington Hill to the Swindon to Aldbourne road. It is one of those enclosed coombes sometimes found in downland, walled in on every side by sloping downs which seem to emphasise their wide skies, shut out all the views, and create an air of expectancy about what exists out of sight over their surrounding slopes. The deer that are frequently seen in Shipley Bottom today are a memory of the deer that ran here when John of Gaunt had his hunting lodge at Upper Upham, a little to the south, and hunted the deer of the area. The east end of Shipley Bottom is closed by the long smoothe mound of Sugar Hill which is sometimes illuminated with a warm and beautiful glow when it catches the evening light at sunset.

The Ridgeway (continued)

Along Whitefield Hill the Ridgeway is to a great extent confined by hedges, but it becomes more open as it approaches its crossing of the Ogbourne to Aldbourne road on Round Hill Downs and the views open out. At Chase Woods (216750) beyond Round Hill Downs the Ridgeway again becomes confined by trees and hedges and it swings from its southerly direction to continue first south-west between hedgerows, and then descend westwards to cross the main road and the tiny River Og at Southend, south of Ogbourne St George. It then (at 194737) continues for half a mile due north until it reaches a metalled road where it turns west again to take the long but gentle

The Og Valley from the Ridgeway on Round Hill Downs

rise of Smeathe's Ridge up to Barbury. From Smeathe's Ridge panoramic views may be enjoyed all round, south across the Marlborough Downs to Martinsell on their southern edge, north to Faringdon and Highworth, and back to Liddington Hill with its clump of trees, now almost four miles away to the north-east.

Barbury Castle

At the east end of Smeathe's Ridge the Ridgeway enters Barbury Castle Country Park at Upper Herdswick where refreshments may be obtained at the bungalow of the Warden. It continues east through the large car park (with its public toilets) and in another half-mile passes through Barbury Castle, a roughly oval Iron Age hillfort to the north of which the Battle of *Beranburh* was fought in 556 AD between the Britons and the West Saxons.

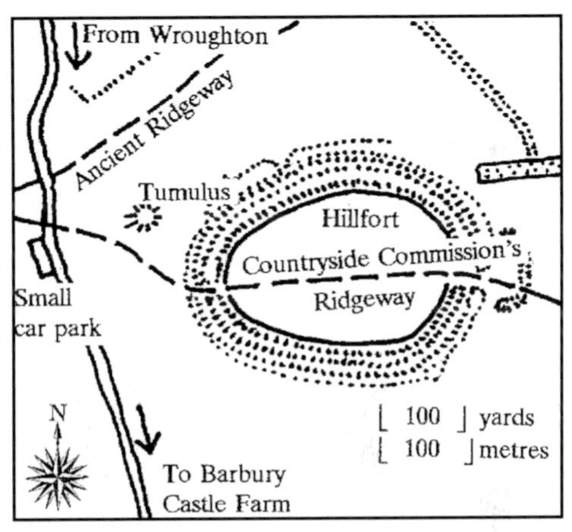

Barbury Castle was, like the Ridgeway in general, an even more wonderful place than it is today in the times when it was less frequented prior to its promotion for recreational purposes and before its urbanisation as a country park. At that time, when Barbury Castle was a lonely hillfort at the north edge of the Marlborough Downs, the forester Rolf Gardiner (1902-1971) who instigated the idea for the Swindon community forest sensed the magic of Barbury. In his chapter headed 'Marching in Downland' from *England Herself: Ventures in Rural Restoration* he relates how at the winter solstice he and his friends would march in downland and how 'Sooner or later these expeditions nearly always veered towards Barbury'. He recalled how 'Of all the downland fortresses Barbury wins the heart', and tells of a winter pilgrimage to Barbury in 1926 when they slept out at midwinter in the vallum of the hillfort.

A short distance east of Barbury Castle car park Burderop Down lies between the ancient Ridgeway crossing the plain to its north and the Countryside Commission's Ridgeway as it climbs the gentle slope of Smeathe's Ridge. On Burderop Down is the Richard Jefferies Memorial (159763), a sarsen stone which was taken fron Fyfield Down and erected as a fitting memorial to Jefferies in 1939. This stone also commemorates Alfred Williams (1877-1930), another local writer associated with these downs which he described as 'sweetly and chastely beautiful' and as 'for ever reflecting the mood of the heavens, and sympathetic to the heart and feelings of man'. Williams was a lesser writer than Richard Jefferies, a working man who was employed on a drop hammer at the Swindon railway factory but managed to educate himself, write poetry and prose, and collect folk songs. Much of his writing was on local history and folklore, some of it about the Marlborough Downs where Barbury Castle was one of his favourite resorts. He was born and died at South Marston, a few miles east of Swindon.

Jefferies' Memorial Stone, Burderop Down

In its progress along Burderop Down this way is marked by a line of Scots pines that were aptly described by Edward Thomas in his biography of Richard Jefferies as resembling a troup of 'titanic wayfarers'.

The Swindon to Marlborough Turnpike

Although most long-distance walkers choose to walk along the Ridgeway, the best walking in the Ridgeway countryside is obtained by getting away from the many walkers (and incidentally the increasing motor traffic) who follow the Ridgeway route now that it has been promoted, and venturing into the countryside which adjoins the Ridgeway. Such walking is available along the turnpike road from Swindon to Marlborough which ran up Ladder Hill at Wroughton and past Burderop Park, Mudgell, Barbury Castle country park and over the downs past Four Mile Clump and Rockley to Marlborough.

This turnpike was opened between 1750 and 1775, long before Swindon expanded as a result of the opening of the Great Western Railway in the 1840s. It is marked by 18th century milestones, one of them immediately south of Four Mile Clump. Between the opening of Marlborough College in 1843 and the construction of the Midland and South Western Junction Railway line to Marlborough through the Ogbournes in the 1870s, the Marlborough schoolboys used to travel across these deserted uplands along this turnpike from Marlborough past Four Mile Clump to Swindon station on Jerry Hammond's horse-drawn bus, Mr Hammond being the enterprising landlord of The Castle and Ball Inn at Marlborough.

Charles Sorley

Four Mile Clump beside this turnpike was a favourite resort of the young poet Charles Hamilton Sorley when he was a schoolboy at Marlborough College. His most anthologised poem 'The song of the ungirt runners' recalls cross-country runs in all winds and weathers in the Marlborough Downs. Sorley, who was a poet of very high promise, wrote most of his poetry at Marlborough College and at the front in the First World War. He loved the Marlborough Downs in rain, wind and sun, and recorded his feelings them in his poem 'Marlborough':

I, who have walked along her downs in dreams,
And known her tenderness and felt her might,
And sometimes by her meadows and her streams
Have drunk deep-storied secrets of delight.

Sorley left Marlborough with deep regret, and spent six months of 1914 at the University of Jena as a student of philosophy. At the outbreak of war he extricated himself from Germany with some difficulty and spent eight hours in a German prison before crossing into Belgium. It is sad to contemplate that had he failed to escape and been interned in Germany he would have escaped the sniper's bullet which ended his life at Loos at the age of twenty.

The Marlborough Turnpike ascending Burderop Down

Hackpen Hill and Glory Ann

After its steep descent from the west end of Barbury Castle the Countryside Commission's Ridgeway diversion rejoins the line of the ancient Ridgeway (at 146764) and runs in an arc to pass over Uffcott Down and climb gently on to Hackpen Hill which is distinguished by its three prominent beech-clumps. From Hackpen, at a height of about 880 feet (268m), there are long views westwards into the flat dairying country around Malmesbury and it is said that here originated the expression 'as different as chalk from cheese', the 'chalk' being the chalk uplands of the Marlborough Downs, and the 'cheese' the clay flatlands to the west where cattle were raised and dairy products made.

Hackpen Hill beech clumps from near Barbury Castle

Celtic folklore frequently refers to fairies inhabiting hills. The Wiltshire antiquary John Aubrey (1626-97) recorded a fairy tale about Hackpen Hill. He related the tale of a shepherd who was lured by a fairy fiddler to a place below Hackpen that resounded with music. It is of interest to note that an area under the escarpment between Broad Hinton and Hackpen Hill is known and is marked by the Ordnance Survey as Fiddler's Hill. This name appears to be a modern one as *The Place-Names of Wiltshire* (1939) ignores the name and it appears on neither the 1773 map by Andrews and Dury nor the first Ordnance Survey of fifty years later.

Bicycle rides to Hackpen Hill from Marlborough College were described in *Summoned by Bells* (1960), the verse autobiography of the former poet laureate Sir John Betjeman (1906-1984).

Further along Hackpen Hill opposite Winterbourne Monkton is the strangely named Glory Ann Pond (128727) which originated as an excavation for brick-earth for the brick kilns shown on the site of Totterdown Woods on old maps. The name has disappeared from the modern maps. Below and east of Glory Ann is Temple Bottom where the Knights Templar had a preceptory in the 12th and 13th centuries. From Glory Ann to the crossing of tracks above Avebury (at 125708) the land east of the Ridgeway is a rock-strewn landscape littered with the sarsen stones that were used to construct Avebury Stone Circle and many buildings in this locality. They are best seen in Fyfield Down Nature Reserve (140707) which is well worth a diversion (east from 125708). This most interesting area situated east of the Ridgeway on Hackpen Hill will be described later (in Chapter 2).

At the point where the way which runs north-east from Avebury as Green Street crosses the Ridgeway (at 125708) the Ridgeway runs merely a mile and a half from the great prehistoric Stone Circle. The village of Avebury is a great centre for walking, a fact which was appreciated by that enthusiastic walker and connoisseur of English landscape Edward Thomas who wrote in his field notebook in 1911: '11 May, Avebury. I never saw such a village for paths etc. round about, all over a space of about a mile – a good book might be written of these paths alone, a very good book'. This note by Thomas was one of the factors that prompted me to write my book on *The Marlborough Downs*.

The Ridgeway on Hackpen Hill, looking north

Silbury Hill

When proceeding south down the Ridgeway along Hackpen Hill, from a point opposite Glory Ann Pond the top terrace of Silbury Hill becomes visible peeping over Waden Hill. It remains in sight for the entire stretch to Overton Hill, generally not readily recognisable as Silbury because only the very top platform of the hill is visible. Whether there is any significance in this fact I am unable to say, although it does not seem to have been recognised before despite endless speculation about the purpose for the construction of Silbury. The reason for the immense amount of effort expended by prehistoric man in the construction of Silbury Hill, the biggest man-made mound in Europe and unusually for an artificial mound designated 'Hill', has never been established.

Water was both essential to life and at a premium in these arid uplands, and it is known that prehistoric tribes often created shrines at river sources. The archaeologist L.V. Grinsell has drawn attention to the cult of worship of springs and wells from prehistoric into medieval times. Silbury is situated beside the Winterbourne stream that feeds the River Kennet near the point where it was augmented by the flow from Swallowhead Springs (101681), a fact which leads me to suggest that one explanation for Silbury is that it may have been constructed as an immense shrine at the joint sources of the River Kennet. It is perhaps significant that on Palm Sundays local people used to congregate on Silbury Hill to drink a mixture of sugar and water taken from Swallowhead Springs, a practice which may have been a survival of prehistoric worship of the water source.

The *Polissoir* Stone

About a hundred and fifty yards east of the Ridgeway towards the south end of Hackpen Hill, near the racing gallops which adjoin the Ridgeway, lies one of the least known and little visited items of archaeological interest in the Marlborough Downs. This is the *polissoir* (French for polisher), a prostrate sarsen stone (128715) used as a sharpening stone by Neolithic man to sharpen stone axes. This stone, which is very difficult to locate, is not marked by the Ordnance Survey and it also escaped the notice of the archaeological gazetteer included in Volume One of the *Victoria County History of Wiltshire*. The *polissoir* has been split by sarsen masons for building stone and a quarter of it has been removed, but fortunately the interesting section which has five grooves used for sharpening the edges of stone axes and the *cuvette* for polishing their faces has survived intact.

Opposite: The Polissoir Stone

Overton Hill

The track from Fyfield Down to Avebury which crosses the Ridgeway on Overton Down (at 125708) was the main road from London to Bristol until the valley road was constructed along the line of the A4 in the early 18th century (more on this subject is included in Chapter 2). From this crossing above Avebury the Ridgeway gently descends for a mile and a half to Overton Hill where the Ridgeway Long Distance Trail ends at the A4. In this descent it crosses the line of the former Roman road a little north of the A4, and on Overton Hill it passes a barrow cemetery containing a number of Bronze Age round barrows. Overton Hill was known to the Anglo-Saxons as *Seofan Beorgas* (Seven Barrows), and it continued to be known as Seven Barrows Hill until the 17th century.

A rather tenuous literary association with this stretch of the Ridgeway is the fact that, when The National Trust acquired land between Avebury and the Ridgeway to protect the environs of the Avebury World Heritage Site, the acquisition of the downland was part financed from the charitable trust set up to distribute the royalties from *The Seven Pillars of Wisdom* by T.E. Lawrence (1888-1935), better known as Lawrence of Arabia.

On Overton Hill the Countryside Commission's Ridgeway long distance trail ends at the A4, although the ancient Ridgeway continues south through East Kennett to cross the Vale of Pewsey and run on south or south-west as described in Chapter 3. Where it ends no one is quite sure for, having reached the prehistoric centre of the Avebury district, it seems to lose much of its purpose.

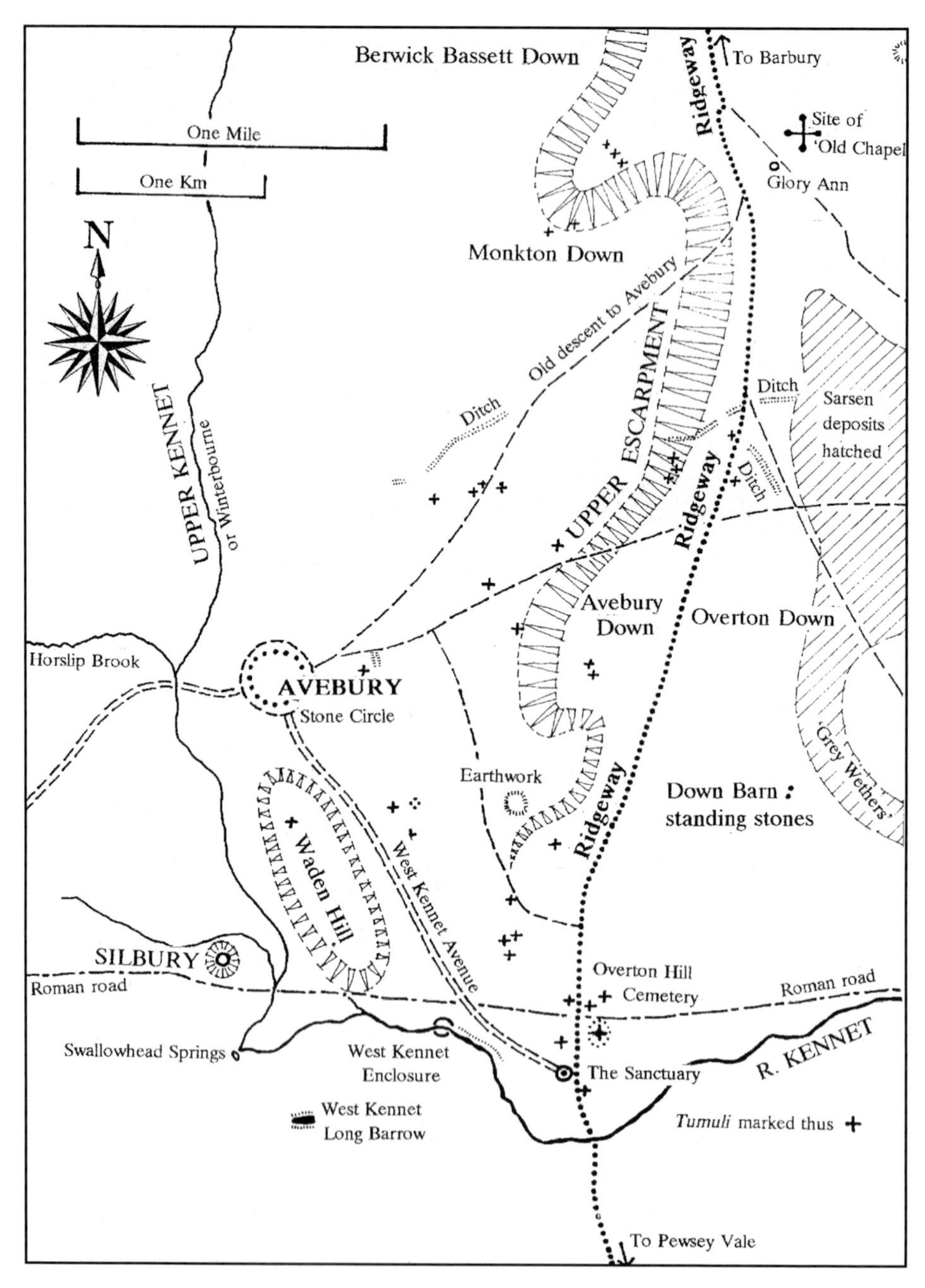

Avebury and Overton Down in prehistoric times

Above: Round barrows beside the Ridgeway on Overton Hill.

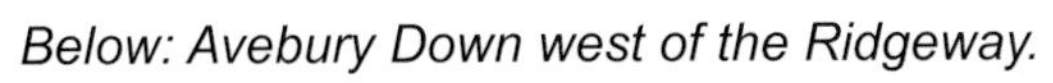

Below: Avebury Down west of the Ridgeway.

Suggested Walks in Ridgeway Country

The linear walking along the Ridgeway requires no further description, having already been effectively described in the chapter above. The walk suggestions which follow are into the countryside closely associated with the Ridgeway. Many of these suggested walks are walks which I have led on many occasions over the last ten years for the Countryside Commission.

1A: Bishopstone to Bishopstone Lynchets (2.5 miles: map 174):
The village of Bishopstone and its lynchets are well worth visiting for the Bishopstone lynchets are one of the least-known significant sights of Wiltshire. The lynchets may easily be reached by parking in Bishopstone village and walking about a mile south (from 247835 on the minor road to Ridgeway Farm) up the coombe to the Ridgeway at 243822. The return may be north-east along the Ridgeway to Ridgeway Farm, then north-west down the track back to Bishopstone.

1B: Fox Hill to Bishopstone and its Lynchets (5 miles: map 174):
A better although slightly more energetic approach is to walk from the small car park (at 233815 on the Ridgeway a little north-east of the Shepherd's Rest Inn at Fox Hill) for a mile north-east along the Ridgeway over Charlbury Hill. Descend down the track (from 243822) which provides a dramatic oblique view along the lynchets into the valley to Bishopstone village. After walking through the village proceed south-east along the minor road (from 247835) towards Ridgeway Farm and Russley Downs and at the farm turn south-west (right) and follow the Ridgeway for a mile and a half back to Fox Hill. An alternative and better return route is achieved by diverging right from the road to Ridgeway Farm immediately after leaving Bishopstone (at 247835) and following the public footpath which runs south up the coombe and under Bishopstone Folly to the Ridgeway and west back to the starting point. This entire walk represents a distance of about 5 miles, to which should be added any distance walked

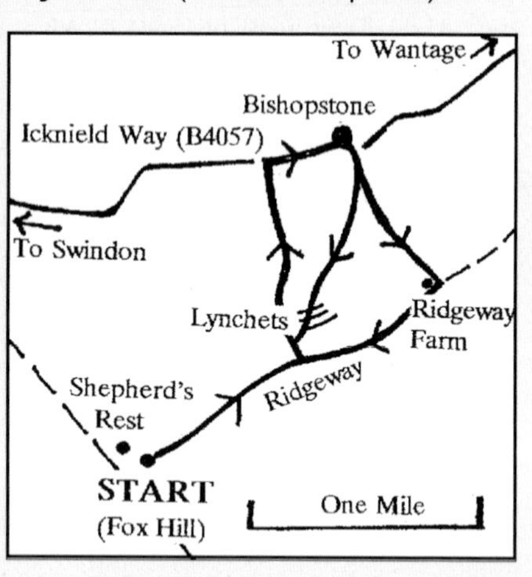

in exploring the village. If this walk is taken on a sunny day and is timed to end late in the day the sun will set ahead behind Liddington Hill during the descent of Charlbury Hill to the Shepherd's Rest.

Despite the presence of the M4 motorway crossing Wanborough Plain a little to its north-east, the area around Snap and Upper Upham provides exceptionally fine walking. Cars may be conveniently parked at either the B4192 at Shipley Bottom (230786), to the north of Liddington Hill, at Woodsend, or on Round Hill Downs (214754). Although there is vehicular access to Upper Upham the parking there is restricted. The elevated viewpoints of the area are at Liddington Hill (277m), Upper Upham (about 260m), and Round Hill Downs (252m). The views from Liddington over the wide plain to its north are magnificent despite the insistent sprawling presence of Swindon. From Round Hill Downs above Ogbourne St George long panoramic views can be enjoyed on a clear day across the full width of the Marlborough Downs, to Martinsell eight miles away on the southern horizon, and to the beech clumps on Hackpen Hill six miles to the west. The walks down the unhedged track from Upper Upham south-east towards Aldbourne, and another east along the byway through Shipley Bottom are not soon forgotten.

1C: Upper Upham to Snap (2.5 miles: map 174):
A short walk to Snap deserted village site may be achieved by walking south from Upper Upham down the Heydown Drove (227766) to the coombe in which Snap was situated. The descent of the droveway provides interesting oblique views along the winding coombe past Lodge Lower Barn east towards Aldbourne – the valley followed by Essex and his army in 1643 – and across the coombe to Woodsend on its ridge above Snap to the south. At the south edge of High Clear Plantation (233767), near the derelict pump house a little to the east along this coombe, is a fine group of hornbeams – a tree not often seen in Wiltshire. From Snap walk west on to the Ridgeway, north to the crossing (213774) above Lower Upham, and then east back to Upper Upham.
An alternative short approach to Snap is from the farm at Woodsend (219762).

1D : Shipley Bottom to Upper Upham and Snap (6 to 8 miles : map 174):

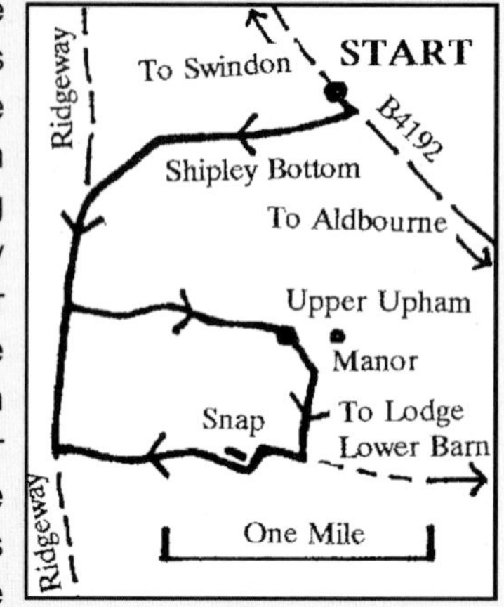

A 6 mile walk which takes in many of the attractions of the Snap and Upham area is achieved by starting from the lay-by on the B4192 road (formerly the A419) which crosses Shipley Bottom (230786), walking west along Shipley Bottom to the Ridgeway Long Distance Trail, south and east to Upper Upham with a short diversion east to see the manor house (at 229772). The Heydown Drove may then be followed south from Upper Upham, turning west (at 227764) through the site of Snap back to the Ridgeway which is then followed north-providing a memorable view of Liddington Hill from the south-to rejoin the outgoing route above Lower Upham (213773) for the return east along Shipley Bottom. This walk may be extended to 8 miles by walking a mile east from the bottom of Heydown Drove (227764) to Lodge Lower Barn (240759) to view the site of the Battle of Aldbourne Chase in the Civil War.

Good walking is available in the broken countryside of Aldbourne Chase south-east of the Ridgeway as it passes through the west end of Chase Woods.

1E: Aldbourne Chase and Sound Bottom (9 miles: map 174) :
A car may be parked on the Ridgeway on Round Hill Downs (215753). A fine nine mile walk may then be taken by walking south-east to Whiteshard Bottom, south-west to the Roman road at 209717, then east past Woodlands Farm and along the former coach road through Sound Bottom. At the east end of Sound Bottom walk a short distance north up the road and at 245716 leave the road and walk west then north-west over the downs back through Whiteshard Bottom and Chase Woods to Round Hill Downs (sketch map overleaf)

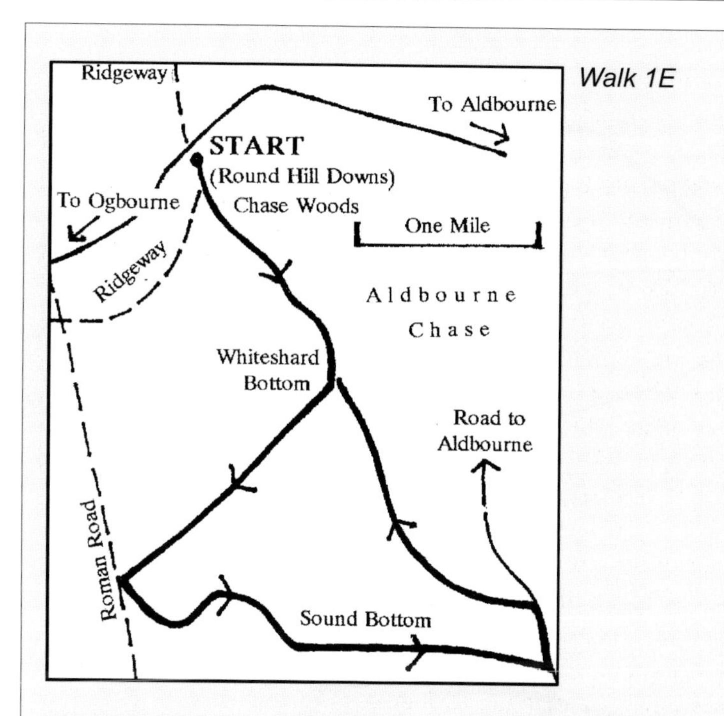

Walk 1E

1F: A Circuit around the Marlborough Downs (11 miles; map 173):
A particularly fine circular walk around the rim of the Marlborough Downs may be taken from Barbury Castle Country Park where there is parking for many cars. Walk first east and be careful to leave the Ridgeway (at 158758) by continuing south-east down the old Marlborough to Swindon turnpike. Soon Four Mile Clump is reached, a high-perched clump of trees (at 165746) which is a landmark for many miles around. The name arises from the fact that the clump is four miles from Marlborough. From Four Mile Clump splendid panoramic views are obtained across the saucer of the Marlborough Downs, to the three Hackpen beech clumps to the west, to Barbury Castle to the north-west, and to Martinsell eight miles away on the southern horizon above the Vale of Pewsey. After continuing down the turnpike to near Old Eagle former inn site (167715) the full circuit of the Marlborough Downs can be completed by turning west through Rockley village and continuing over Manton Down and the prehistoric field systems and sarsen stones of Fyfield and Overton Downs (described in Chapter 2) to the Ridgeway. The Ridgeway is then followed, north along Hackpen Hill and then east through Barbury Castle hillfort back to the car park (map overleaf).

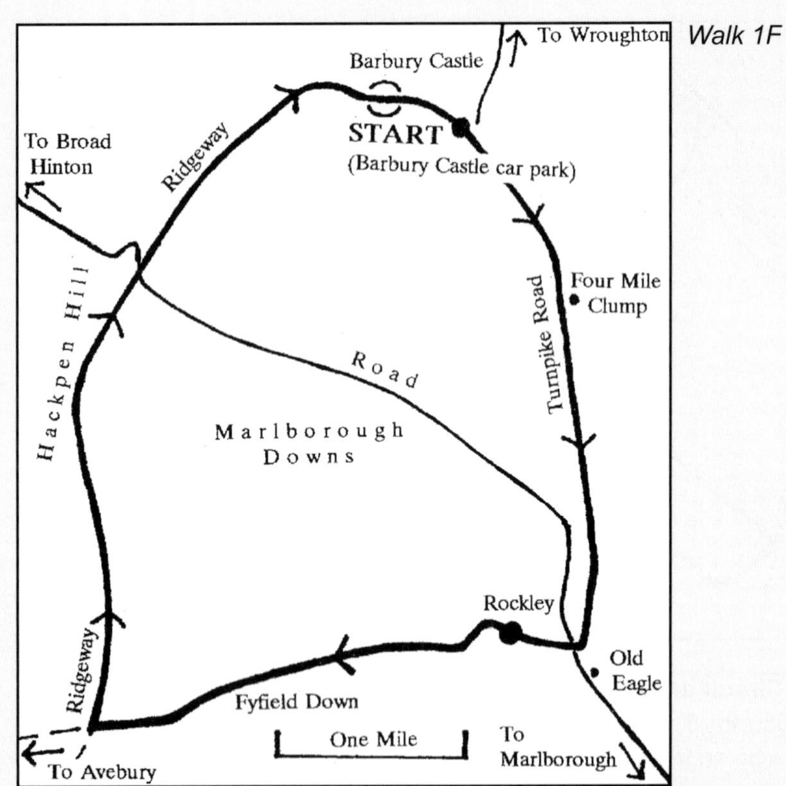

Walk 1F

1G: Smeathe's Ridge and Burderop Down (5 miles: map 173): Another walk east from Barbury is down the glorious unhedged grassy descent of Smeathe's Ridge (170756) with its splendid views, to near Ogbourne St George. From Barbury Castle car park walk east and after about a hundred yards take care to fork left away from the turnpike and descend Smeathe's Ridge. At 189746 double back along the footpath which runs north-west and at 171764 turn west and climb on to Burderop Down. In returning west to Barbury car park the track passes the Richard Jefferies Memorial (159762), a standing sarsen stone erected in 1939. As it passes the Jefferies Memorial the track runs above extensive prehistoric field systems that extend over almost a hundred and fifty acres, and a medieval enclosure (160764) on the north face of Burderop Down, all of which are best seen from the former coach road near Mudgell (map opposite).

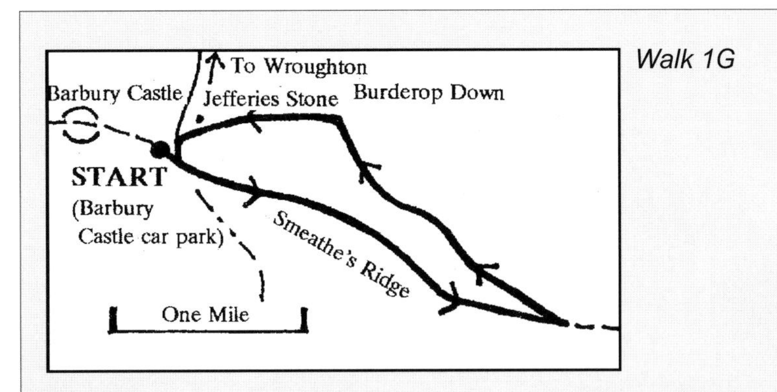

Walk 1G

Many other walks associated with the Ridgeway are available east of Hackpen Hill. Some of the best of these are described in Chapter 2 ('The Central Marlborough Downs').

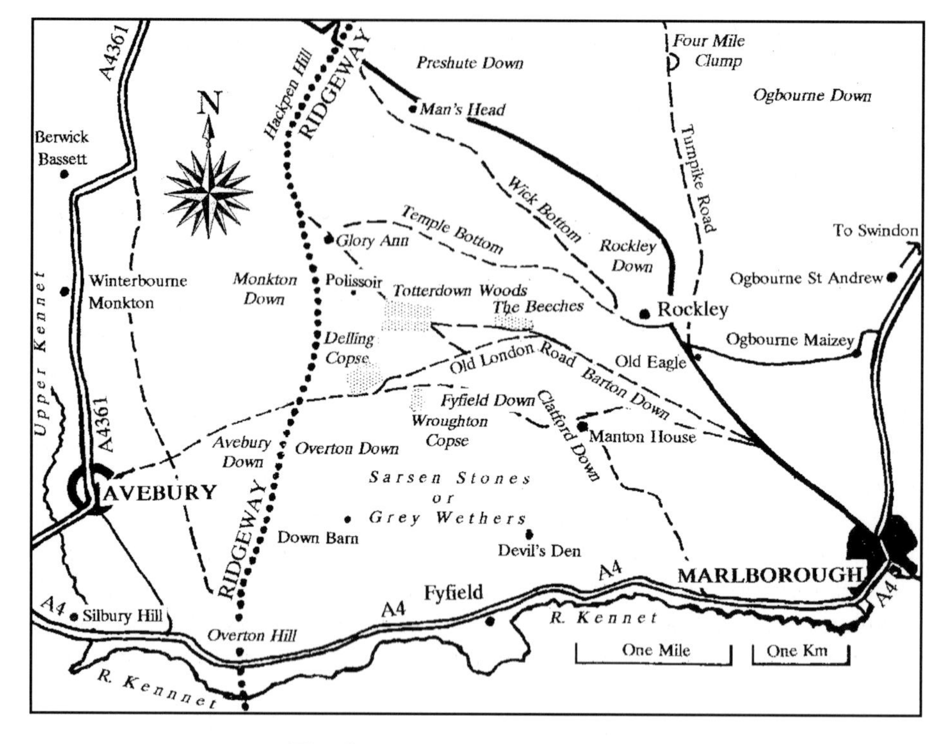

The Central Marlborough Downs

2 The Central Marlborough Downs

Fyfield and Overton Downs, Glory Ann, Temple and Wick Bottoms

(map Landranger 173)

Immediately to the east of the Ridgeway as it follows the escarpment along Hackpen Hill lies an area, designated for the purpose of this chapter the Central Marlborough Downs, to distinguish it from the extremities of the Marlborough Downs which reach north-east to Bishopstone and south-west towards Devizes. This area is in reality part of the 'Ridgeway Country' described in Chapter 1, but it is of such great interest that this entire chapter has been devoted to it. The district is an area of utterly unspoilt chalk downland landscape which is particularly rich in archaeological and historical associations, and it offers a quality of walking that is unsurpassed in Wiltshire.

It is a district which possesses a character which justifies Thomas Hardy's description of Wessex, which included the Marlborough Downs, as a 'partly real, partly dream country'. The Marlborough based poet Charles Hamilton Sorley picked up this dreamy aspect of these downs when he wrote in his poem 'Marlborough': 'I who have walked along her downs in dreams', and Edward Thomas came very near Hardy's 'partly dream country' when he wrote of this area in his critical biography of the local Victorian writer Richard Jefferies: 'In his home country we are in a spirit land'.

Most of the multitudes of visitors who throng Avebury never leave the village and depart satisfied that they have seen all that is of interest, quite unaware that they have missed seeing the essential remote landscape associated with Avebury some of which lies over the ridge to the east of the village and provides the atmospheric setting for the World Heritage Site. It is doubtful whether one in a hundred visitors to Avebury enter this area which is one of the most glorious areas for walking in Wiltshire. It is the area described by Edward Thomas as 'a beautiful, a quiet, an unrenowned, and a most visibly ancient land', with 'a hugeness of undivided surface for which there is no comparison to be made on earth'. Richard Jefferies described it as being alive with the dead', and Professor Fowler has described the landscape of Overton and Fyfield Downs as containing 'a better preserved area of earthworks than any other in Wessex'.

The area of which I write lies midway between Avebury and the tiny village of Rockley and is bounded on its west by the historic Ridgeway. It is a fascinating area parts of which resemble a rock-strewn landscape of Cornwall rather than a chalk downland in the heart of Wiltshire. Since 1956 part of this area amounting to 612 acres has been designated the Fyfield Down National Nature Reserve and is administered on a 99-year lease by the Nature Conservancy Council. It consists generally of unimproved chalk grassland which is of considerable biological interest. Geological interest is provided by the surface deposits of sarsen stones.

Fyfield and Overton Downs

Most English landscapes have been influenced by the activities of man over the ages, but here at Fyfield Down and Overton Down the archaeology lies so thick on the ground that we have effectively a man-made landscape which was investigated and excavated by Professor P.J. Fowler in the 1960s. Throughout the ages until comparatively modern times man has settled here and left his marks upon the landscape, from Neolithic man with his long barrows through the Bronze Age when men were selecting and transporting the sarsens from here for the monuments at Avebury – and perhaps for Stonehenge – through the Iron Age with its 'Celtic' field sytems to the Romano-Britons who settled towards the south end of the area at Down Barn and elsewhere. This was discovered by Professor Fowler in the early 1960s and subsequently from aerial photographs taken during the exceptionally dry summer of 1995 which revealed unsuspected Romano-British settlement sites in this upland area. It is also likely that activities on these downs continued in post-Roman times, and that they were also taken over by the Saxons in the 5th and 6th centuries, for the Saxons were in the Kennet Valley at Fyfield and Overton, their parishes run up into the downs over this area, and a pagan Saxon pot was found in the 19th century near Temple Farm in Temple Bottom.

Nevertheless, since the Saxons were basically valley dwellers, it is likely that during the Anglo-Saxon period the downland settlements weakened, to be revived in early medieval times when a farmstead owned by the Priory of St Swithin at Winchester existed south of Wroughton Copse (138707). A settlement of the same date existed in the copse known as The Beeches (147717), and there was a Templar presence in Temple Bottom.

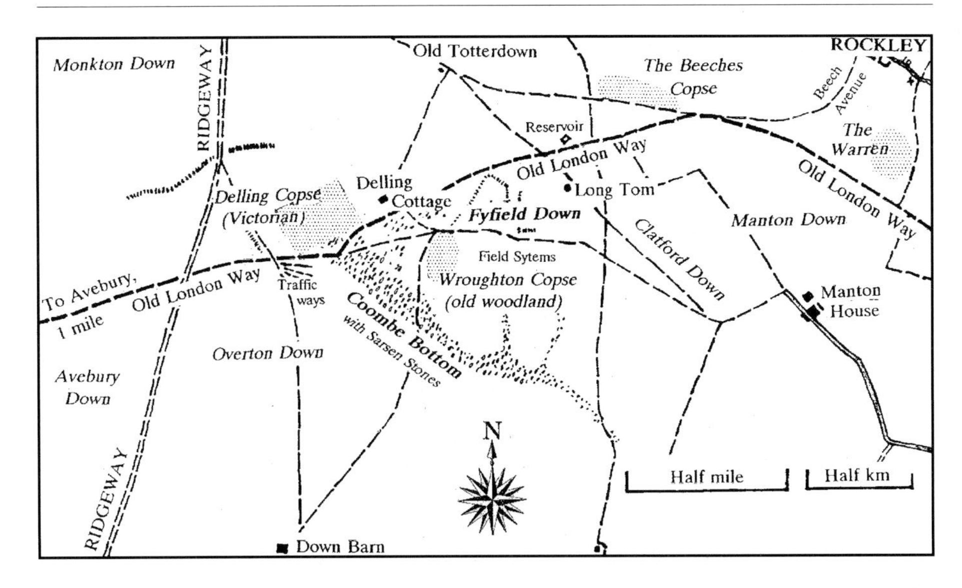

The extent of monastic occupation of these Marlborough Downlands in the early Middle Ages – with the Priory of Ogbourne at Ogbourne, Stanley Abbey at Wick Bottom, the Knights Templar in Temple Bottom, the Priory of St Swithin at Wroughton Copse, and Clatford Priory in the Kennet Valley to the immediate south – has never to my knowledge been fully recognised. At some time, probably during this monastic presence here in the 12th century, these uplands were abandoned to sheep and probably depopulated, although in the 17th century a farmstead operated for a time a little south of Delling Copse (at 133707). Rabbits were at some unknown date introduced around Delling and rabbit-warrening and sporting activities were pursued until early in the present century when racehorses finally superseded the rabbits.

Parallel with the sporting and warrening activities the sarsen cutting which provided dense stone for building purposes and was carried on from about 1840 to 1940. Today the only human habitations in these downs are the cottage at New Totterdown and several dwellings in Temple and Wick Bottoms. More than any other district of Wiltshire this now deserted landscape is utterly redolent of the past, and the area is left to the grazing of sheep and cattle, to racehorse training, and to brooding over its historic past.

'Celtic' Field Systems

'Celtic' field systems survive on Fyfield Down (around 140712) as lynchet banks up to 8 feet (2.4m) high at the edge of prehistoric fields. These banks built up on these gentle slopes as the result of sarsen stones being removed from the fields to allow them to be ploughed and gathered at the edges of the fields. A combination of ploughing and weathering then gradually displaced the topsoil down the slopes and its movement was checked by these stones which effectively revetted the banks as over hundreds of years they slowly built up with accumulated topsoil. Pottery sherds in the field banks suggest that the fields were in use from the Bronze Age, through the Iron Age, and well into the Romano-British period when the Romans settled at the south end of Overton Down near Down Barn (130695) and at several other sites in this area.

Although not evident on the ground, a considerable Bronze Age presence in the Marlborough Downs in the form of distributed farmsteads has recently been ascertained from aerial photography, and it is probable that the Iron Age field systems of Fyfield Down were successors to earlier fields dating from the Bronze Age.

Towards the end of the Roman period it appears that much of the Fyfield Down arable field systems was given over to grazing. The use as pasture probably continued beyond Anglo-Saxon times, for there is evidence of 4th, 5th and 10th century settlement on Fyfield Down, followed by a 12th and 13th century settlement with long houses – that is long barn-like buildings shared by humans and stock animals-south of Wroughton Copse (138707). The existence of a 17th century farmstead has already been noted south of Delling Copse (133707). This farmstead seems to have been the last occupation by human beings of these downs, apart from a pair of cottages at Glory Ann (128727) which were occupied into the 19th century, the isolated cottages occupied by warreners and gamekeepers at Delling (135712) and Old Totterdown (138718) which were inhabited until recently, the house at New Totterdown (131721), and the farms and dwellings in Temple and Wick Bottoms which remain occupied today.

A number of standing stones of indefinite date exist in these downs. One of these stones, a tall slender stone located to the east of Fyfield Down between two racing gallops and known as Long Tom (145713), is 8 feet (2.4m) high and is now partly concealed by an elder bush which makes it easily missed. This stone was probably a parish boundary marker in these featureless uplands. Others may be more modern stones marking the boundaries of its former owners the Meux estate.

Left: Long Tom on Clatford Down

Right: Standing stone near Delling Copse

The London to Bath Road

Up to the mid-18th century when the valley road along the line of the A4 was constructed, the main road from London to Bristol and Bath crossed Overton and Fyfield Downs. It left Marlborough over Barton Down and Manton Down and crossed Fyfield Down between Wroughton Copse (138709) and Delling Copse (132711), although the latter, being a Victorian planting to shelter game, did not then exist. At the point where the London Road rose out of the head of Clatford Bottom near Delling Copse to cross Overton Down its traffic ruts can still be seen at The Gangway (132709) fanning out up the slope of the down in an attempt to find better going after the main way had been cut up by the traffic. The fact that the traffic ruts run into Delling Copse proves the late date of the copse. The road continued across the Ridgeway to enter Avebury by Green Street. This was probably the way by which the stones for Avebury were manhandled to construct the stone circle in prehistoric times.

Traffic ruts of the former London Coach Road rising up Overton Down at The Gangway beside Delling Copse (right).

In its course over these remote downs this particularly desolate and dangerous stretch of the coach road would have been followed by most of London society on its way to take the waters at Bath prior to the construction of the lower road along the Kennet Valley. It remains bleak in bad weather even today and few travellers have left accounts of their journey across these downs because at that time wild country was regarded with awe and horror, although in his diary for 15 June 1668 Samuel Pepys (1633-1703) wrote a short description of this landscape which he saw on his return to London after visiting Bath and Bristol:

> It was prodigious to see how full the downs are of great stones, and all along the valleys stones of considerable bigness most of them growing certainly out of the ground so thick as to cover the ground.

A few years later, in his story 'A Step to Bath' (1700), Ned Ward tells of leaving Marlborough by coach in some apprehension about a warning that 'a party of Light Horse [highwaymen] lay hidden, perchance to ease us out of our Rhino [valuables]'. He also relates how the passengers suffered 'confused jolts' from the many stones along the way.

Old London Road east of Fyfield Down above Rockley

Sarsen Stones

The Wiltshire writer Geoffrey Grigson loved this area which he aptly described as a 'land of sheep and sarsens'. The sarsen stones which formerly covered the area far more densely than they do today were utilised in prehistoric times for stone circles and isolated standing stones, and for the chambers of long barrows such as those at West Kennett and The Devil's Den (153696) in Clatford Bottom not far from the A4. Prehistoric man has moved many of the sarsens to clear areas for agriculture, and these stones are consequently sometimes arranged at field edges into straight alignments known as 'sarsen trains'.

From the medieval period the sarsens were in demand for building stone and paving, and in about 1840 the sarsen masons from Buckinghamshire, who had been excavating buried sarsen, heard of the surface deposits of sarsen which existed here and moved to Wiltshire. From about 1840 to 1940 familes such as the Frees and Cartwrights exploited the deposits of sarsen, squaring them into blocks for building stone and road setts. This explains the depletion of the stones from the time when it was said that it was possible to walk the length of Clatford Bottom from Delling to the main road along the valley (now the A4) stepping only on sarsen stones.

Many of the surviving sarsen stones have been moved or split by the stone cutters, and at least one has a splitting wedge left embedded in its surface. The stone cutters often suffered from silicosis and exposure from their activities on these high downs and tended to die young. Their gravestones can be found in the local graveyards, for example that of Edward Free, who died aged forty-five in 1875, in Fyfield churchyard.

The name sarsen is said to have originated in medieval times when the Saracens were well-known as foreigners and their name was applied to these apparently alien sandstones in a limestone district. The name may however – and this perhaps seems more likely – have developed from the Anglo-Saxon *sar* meaning troublesome and *stan* meaning stone, the sarsens having proved a great hindrance to agriculture. Their local name of Grey Wethers which arises from their resemblence at a distance to a flock of sheep and has gained credence from being applied to them by the Ordnance Survey on its maps. The stones vary greatly in colour from a leaden grey to a rich orange-red, and their texture from a silky smootheness to a pitted roughness. Many are holed by the root runs of trees which existed at the time that

Sarsen stones on Overton Down

the stone was laid down. Fyfield Down Nature Reserve is particularly notable for the rich variety of lichens which embellish its sarsen stones, calling to mind two lines by George Crabbe (1754-1832), the poet who was an amateur geologist, became a Wiltshire vicar at Trowbridge, and described the patina on stones as:

The living stains, which Nature's hand alone,
Profuse of life, pours out upon the stones.

Since they are sandstones, sarsens create an individual flora in this otherwise calcareous district as a result of the localised acidification resulting from the acidic run-off from their surfaces. In spring the richly coloured splodges of lichen on the sarsens are complemented by the yellow of gorse blooms and the blue of bluebells among the scrub growth and the sheep.

Rabbit Warrening

By the late 19th century Overton Down and Fyfield Down, being rendered useless for agriculture because of the obstruction caused by the sarsen stones, were managed as a gigantic rabbit warren. The warrener's lodge was at Delling Cottage (135713) which still survives beside a circle of beech trees east of Delling Copse. In an adjacent shed, the rabbits were gutted before being sent by the cartload to the London dealers whose receipts for rabbits from this area still exist.

Delling Cottage (the former warren lodge) and its attendant beech circle.

When, in the early 1900s, the rabbit holes proved to be hazardous to the valuable racehorses which were trained in the area it was decided that the rabbits must go and Mr Bull, their former warrener, was paid by the trainer Mr Alec Taylor to dispose of his former charges. Today, racehorse training gallops run down a line east of the Ridgeway and west of Overton Down, and also occupy the south-east of Fyfield Down towards the substantial training establishment at Manton House.

H.J. Massingham, when writing his *English Downland* in 1936, was particularly interested in the area, which he called 'the Valley of the Desolation of the Rocks' and described as 'strewn with a multitude of sarsen stones, great and small and half embedded in the sweet turf: There is no wilder place in all Wiltshire, though but a mile or so from the Bath Road'. I can only think from his use of the word 'desolation' that Massingham was at Fyfield Down on a glowering day for having visited this remote area on innumerable occasions, and often alone, I find it a benign and hospitable landscape with which I feel a close affinity and in which I have no feelings of desolation and feel utterly at ease.

The gently undulating terrain of Fyfield and Overton Downs provides a varied landscape. The sarsen-littered coombe between the two downs – it seems perverse that the higher parts are called downs, but the term derives from the Anglo-Saxon *dun* meaning hill – is enclosed by low sloping shoulders of down which block out the views, but upon climbing the short distance to

Parting of the ways on Overton Down with the Old London Way to the left.

the higher points vast panoramic views open up in all directions, to Barbury Castle in the north, to Four Mile Clump in the north-east, Savernake Forest in the east, to Martinsell and the hills of the Pewsey Vale occupying the southern horizon six miles away, and west over Avebury to the slender obelisk of the Lansdowne Monument above Cherhill.

At the coombe bottom between Overton and Fyfield Downs the way from Avebury divides (133709) opposite Delling Copse and both branches pick their way through the multitude of sarsen boulders and juniper, gorse and thorn scrub. The left branch veers away as a gravelled track, climbs out of the coombe and passes through the Fyfield Down prehistoric field systems on its way above Rockley to Marlborough and London. The other branch, which continues straight on as a grassy green way and passes left of Wroughton Copse, provides an alternative way to Marlborough past Manton House.

From the point where the south-west corner of Delling Copse is reached on Overton Down the field banks of the Fyfield Down prehistoric field systems are visible ahead. On the immediate left is Delling Copse, and in the middle distance slightly right is Wroughton Copse. To the right is a glorious view south-east down the coombe of Clatford Bottom, which with its dense scatter of sarsen stones resembles a boulder-strewn stream bed, to the Devil's Den dolmen just visible beside a barn a mile and a half away, and beyond to Martinsell on the south-eastern horizon. The Dorset writer Thomas Hardy (1840-1928) wrote a story entitled 'What the Shepherd Saw' located at the Devil's Den. Nearer on the right along the ridge of Overton Down is the fenced ditch and bank, with a row of rods projecting out of the ridge of its bank, of the experimental earthwork (130706) which was constructed in 1960 to monitor the effects of weathering and erosion on a man-made earthwork.

In *Round About Wiltshire* (1907) A.G.Bradley mentioned on some undisclosed authority that when Charles I was at Marlborough his army camped 'on the down about Fyfield'. If this is true it must have been north of the village, probably on Fyfield Hill at the south end of Fyfield Down, west of the Devil's Den, and north-east of Piggle Dean where The National Trust has preserved a coombe beside the A4 containing many sarsen stones. Mr Bradley's suggestion is supported by the fact that a Civil War soldier called Symons left an account of the sarsen stones of this district which he may have seen when encamped above Fyfield.

Wroughton Copse Farmstead

The early-medieval monastic farmstead which existed a little south of Wroughton Copse on Fyfield Down (at 138707) during the 12th and 13th centuries is generally known as Wroughton Copse Settlement and sometimes as Wroughton Mead. It consisted of a 12-acre embanked enclosure containing three smaller enclosures and four buildings. It is associated with extensive medieval ridge-and-furrow which shows up distinctly on aerial photographs as overlying the prehistoric field systems of the area. The fact that the substantial area of medieval broad ridge-and-furrow to the north, north-east, and east of Wroughton Copse respected the settlement implies that it was probably contemporary with it.

Sarsen litter between Overton Down and Fyfield Down with Wroughton Copse at centre.

In the surviving records of the Priory of St Swithins at Winchester the Wroughton Copse farmstead is named *Raddun*, meaning 'red down', the name originating from the red clay-with-flints that here overlays the chalk downland. These records reveal that wheat was grown and cattle and hens were kept, but the farmstead was principally devoted to sheep husbandry. During the 1960s Professor Fowler excavated this farmstead and found that its four buildings included a 60 foot long combined dwelling house and byre (a 'long house'), all within the north-east segment of the encircling earthwork. His interim reports appeared in *Wiltshire Archaeological Magazine* (Volume 58). Finds established occupation from about 1100 to 1300, a period which is contemporary with the Templar presence at Temple Rockley a little to its north which will be described later in this chapter.

An early-medieval settlement of similar date to Wroughton Copse (12th to 13th century) existed at The Beeches (149717), now a copse with a rough wall of large sarsens situated three-quarters of a mile north-east of the Wroughton Copse farmstead towards Temple Bottom. The dating of The Beeches is established from the pottery found when it was excavated in 1949. The communities which existed in this central area of the Marlborough Downs contrived to survive far from any constant running water. The nearest rivers are the Winterbourne or Upper Kennet three miles to the west, the River Kennet a few miles to the south, and the River Og several miles to the east, although the Hungerbourne (also known as Hunger Brook) occasionally rises near Rockley and runs down to join the River Og at Bay Bridge. This winterbourne used to arise only after very wet autumns, when it would flood the road at Old Eagle. A document of 1776 in the Wiltshire Record Office records a proposal to re-route the highway at Rockley because of flooding, and some of the farm buildings in the village have apertures at the foot of their walls to allow the Hungerbourne through, but today the lowering of the water table has ensured that the winterbourne appears less frequently than in the past, when it was believed to presage a disaster. There was an exceptional rising of the Hungerbourne in 1960 which was said to have been the first since 1915, and it rose again in 1977.

A great deal of time may be enjoyably spent wandering over this fascinating landscape of Fyfield and Overton Downs which I believe to be one of the most enjoyable and least known major landscapes of Wiltshire. Despite having visited this part of Wiltshire on literally hundreds of occasions, at all seasons and in all types of weather, I find that its attractions never pall and there is always something of interest to be seen. Wide views are obtained from the high points, the shallow coombes offer seclusion, are sun-traps on a warm day and provide shelter from the wind on a boisterous day. The public are restricted to the rights of way in the nature reserve, but Fyfield and Overton Downs are very well served with footpaths which offer many alternative routes.

Temple Bottom and the Knights Templar

Occasionally the place-name 'Temple' crops up in the English countryside. It almost invariably indicates that in the early Middle Ages an estate in the area where the name occurs was owned by the Knights Templar. In the dry coombe known as Temple Bottom (143725) north of Fyfield Down a whole rash of Temple names appears on the map including Temple Farm, Temple Covert and Temple Bottom Farm. At some time between 1155 and 1159 the Knights Templar were granted a preceptory in or near Temple Bottom by John FitzGilbert, the husband of Sibyl the sister of the Earl of Salisbury, the former owner of these lands. There were two estates in this area, Langdon Wick based on Wick Bottom (146734) which runs parallel to Temple Bottom, and Temple Rockley, the Templar estate based on Temple Bottom which was entirely divorced from the village of Rockley, being in another parish.

A long arm of Preshute parish extends north up the western boundary of the parish of Ogbourne St George and consequently the west ends of both Temple Bottom and Wick Bottom are in Preshute parish, but their eastern ends run into the parish of Ogbourne St Andrew which also contains Rockley village. Both Langdon Wick and Temple Rockley were tithings of Preshute parish. At Domesday Temple Rockley was in the possession of the Earl of Salisbury, although by 1159 it had been conveyed to the Templars.

In the early 14th century the Monastic Order of the Knights Templar was suppressed by Pope Clement V at the instigation of Philip IV of France who coveted their extensive estates. As a result of a 'bull' issued by the pope in 1309 several Templars including their leader Walter de Ruckley (Rockley) were arrested and imprisoned by the Constable of Marlborough Castle who was ordered to transfer them from Marlborough Castle to the Tower of London, and that is the last we hear of them.

The 1308-9 survey of Templar lands at the Public Record Office reveals that at Temple Rockley there was a large establishment consisting of a refectory, a hall, kitchen, chamber, bakehouse, brewhouse and chapel. There were by then no longer any Templars living at Rockley, presumably due to their suppression.

The location of the Templar preceptory at Temple Rockley has never to my knowledge been adequately researched. It has always been assumed to have been at or near Temple Farm (137727) in Temple Bottom, but its precise location has never been positively established. Temple Farm is now confusingly situated at the place formerly known as Top Temple, a second Temple Farm having now appeared at the site formerly known as Temple Bottom Barn (148724). On their 1773 map of Wiltshire, Andrews and Dury show Temple Farm as 'The Temple', a name by which many of the larger

Templar establishments were known, including those in Paris and London. Sheep husbandry was practised at Temple Rockley where it is recorded that sheep were milked to make cheese.

The fact that a Templar Knight once expressed his frustration at being posted to England by exclaiming: 'We are preceptors of sheep!' suggests that sheep farming must have been widely practised by the Templars in England. In the 13th century sheep were extensively farmed on monastic estates principally for their wool, their skins from which parchment was made, and for their milk which was made into cheese. Sheep meat was then of little consequence, but in connection with the wide practice by the Templars of sheep husbandry it should be noted that at all times Templars were required by their order to wear sheepskin drawers as well as a white lambskin girdle to remind them of their vows of chastity.

The Knights Templar were at Temple Rockley for only a little over a hundred and fifty years, from about 1155 until their order was suppressed in the early 14th century. Excavation of preceptories of the Knights Templar undertaken elsewhere have revealed that these establishments often took the form of large walled enclosures containing many farm buildings. No evident signs of such an enclosure exist in Temple Bottom, but beside the footpath which runs from Glory Ann down to Wick Bottom and just over the brow of the hill from Temple Bottom an extensive earthwork exists south-west of Wick Down Farm (at 135733) 700 yards (640 m) from Temple Farm. From its situation towards the floor of the coombe and its rectangular nature with square corners, this earthwork appears to be medieval, and so it has proved to be. The *Victoria County History for Wiltshire* (Volume 1, Part 1) schedules it under Wick Down Farm as a rectangular 2.5-acre enclosure of medieval date, and in the *Wiltshire Archaeological Magazine* (Volume 38) for 1913-1914 the Reverend E.H. Goddard described this enclosure:

> Just S. of Wick Farm an oblong enclosure with banks in which sarsen stones are imbedded, other banks and cultivation marks around it [about 100 feet of one of the banks about 1ft. 6ins. high, of the enclosure, removed 1913, when medieval or modern pottery was found under the bank].

The 1900 25-inch Ordnance Survey shows the Wick Down Farm enclosure as it was before the removal of part of its banks in 1913. Its straight south side is shown measuring about 150 yards (164m) and its straight west side about 90 yards (98m). Its north side was double-splayed, and from its irregular east side run two banks, one north-west to a small pond, the other running north-east is sarsen lined. The latter is now followed by a post and rail timber fence running towards the farm. The public footpath from Glory Ann to Wick Down Farm approximately follows the southern edge of the enclosure. The scale of the surviving banks of this earthwork is similar to those surrounding the nearby Wroughton Copse farmstead which is known to be of 12th-13th century date.

The situation of the Wick Down Farm earthwork is an attractive sheltered one on the lee side of the hill from the prevailing wind. The name of 'The Village' which is given to the fields containing this earthwork on the Wick Down Farm estate maps may have arisen from speculation about the earthwork, or it may preserve a tradition of extensive buildings having existed on the site. The earthwork could be the site of a former grange of Stanley Abbey, but it could alternatively have been a Templar establishment and perhaps the Temple Rockley preceptory, for it is known that the Templars sometimes set up villages at their preceptories, for example in Lincolnshire. Once settled, inhabited sites often continue to be occupied, and today the buildings adjoining the medieval enclosure consist of the substantial group including Wick Down Farmhouse, several other dwellings, and many stable blocks and farm buildings.

The two coombes known as Wick Bottom and Temple Bottom are separated by a down known as Rough Hill or Down (134729). The boundary between the Langdon Wick estate and the Temple Rockley estate is now difficult to establish, and it is possible that the latter may formerly have extended over the brow of Rough Hill towards Wick Down Farm. In the context of this suggestion of the possible presence of the Templars at Wick as well as at Temple Bottom, it should be mentioned that in 1194 Langdon Wick was granted to Stanley Abbey, the Cistercian nunnery founded between Chippenham and Calne in 1154. This was the year before the Templars were given Temple Rockley by Richard I who was on good terms with the Templars and co-operated with them in his obsessive Crusading activities for which he neglected his English kingdom and almost lost it to his brother John. There could have been an arrangement for Stanley Abbey when granted Langdon Wick in 1194 to allow the Templars, who were already established in the adjoining Temple Bottom, to farm Langdon Wick as well as Temple Bottom.

The occasional sighting of hobbies in this area – I have seen them at the west end of Temple Bottom towards Glory Ann – are a reminder of the times when the Templars would have used birds of prey for hawking over this countryside. Tradition allocated specific hawks to persons of different status, and the hobby was regarded as being the appropriate hawk for a young man.

The situation of the Wroughton Copse farmstead described earlier (page

61), and its abandonment at about the time that the Templars were suppressed, raises the inevitable question of whether it could have been connected with the Knights Templar at Temple Rockley, or were the Templars and the farmers at Wroughton Copse merely neighbours? In this context it is relevant to note that this farmstead is situated midway between Temple Rockley and the Templar lands at Lockeridge, and that although a man called Richard was in possession of the Wroughton Copse farmstead in 1248, by 1267 and for fifty years after (to about 1317) it was in different ownership, being described as 'late Richard of Raddon's'. The date of about 1317 when Richard's ownership ended practically coincides with the suppression of the Templars. It is also interesting to note that the perimeter banks of the enclosure at Wroughton Copse are of similar scale to those of the medieval earthwork beside Wick Down Farm, and that a spur was found in a cess-pit in one of the buildings at Wroughton Copse.

Templar's Bath in Temple Bottom

An interesting and little known possible relic of the Templars survives in Temple Bottom one mile west-north-west from Rockley south west of the modern house. About thirty yards south of the track along Temple Bottom and on a little green between the house and its tennis court, lies (at 143725) a sarsen stone, the top surface of which has been artificially hollowed out into a large depression with a drainage hole bored through about two feet of solid sarsen. The stone is very large, measuring by my estimation about 15 feet by 10 feet (4.6m by 3m). It was noted by A.D. Passmore in 1924 (*Wiltshire Archaeological Magazine* 51) as being known locally as the Templar's Bath. Its purpose is not known. It may once have served some utilitarian purpose for holding liquid or in connection with cheese-making in these practically waterless downs. Alternatively it may have been used in Templar rituals or as a baptismal trough, perhaps housed in a timber building which has now perished.

The practice of bathing was of eastern origin and among oriental peoples was often a religious rite which it might be expected that the Templars would have brought back from their activities in the east, but Templars were in fact forbidden by their monastic rule to bathe. It is of interest to note that the Reverend Gilbert White in the 18th century discovered a similar large hollowed-out stone in Chapel Field near Selborne in Hampshire, near the former Knights Templar establishment at Temple Manor. When he discovered the Selborne stone it was being used as a hog trough, but in *The Antiquities of Selborne* (Letter XXV) he speculated that it had once been a baptismal font.

During the latter half of the 19th century and up to about 1905 when the stone became exhausted, the sarsen stones of Wick and Temple Bottoms were worked by the Cartwright family of sarsen cutters. The survival of the large and accessible Templar's Bath stone seems to indicate that it was at that time recognised to be of historical importance.

Glory Ann

Of the many walkers who follow the Ridgeway along Hackpen Hill I have noticed on innumerable visits that few turn aside to visit an interesting site which lies a little east of the track (at 128727). This place, which was for long known by the intriguing name of Glory Ann, consists of two hilltop ponds at an altitude of about 876 feet (267m) on Rough Hill above the head of Temple Bottom. Everyone enjoys a mystery and derivation of the name the name Glory Ann presents something of an enigma. *The Place-Names of Wiltshire* mentions 'Glory Ann Barn' but makes no attempt to explain the origin of the name. Ponds at the tops of hills always create interest, as for example in the nursery rhyme when 'Jack and Jill went *up* the hill to fetch a pail of water', and the existence of ponds at high level in otherwise arid downlands led to the myth of dewponds being entirely replenished with dew, although the dewpond theory has now been effectively demolished by a number of authorities.

The largest of the ponds at Glory Ann survives and contains plenty of water having been dredged in 1989, but the secondary pond has now almost disappeared. It is relevant to note that the 1900 Ordnance Survey marks 'Glory Ann Barn' and by labelling the pond 'Old Clay Pit' confirms that the biggest pond was a 'brickhole' excavated in the clay-with-flints capping to the chalk downs when bricks were made in this area at the 'Wroughton Brick Kiln' marked by Andrews and Dury in Totterdown Woods on their 1773 map. The smaller pond, which seems to have originated as a normal pond for watering stock, is partly replenished by overflow from the larger pond.

Glory Ann Pond

A site beside the ponds at Glory Ann was occupied by two cottages and a barn, the barn standing a little north of the ponds where some rubble still exists. A cottage was mentioned by Colt Hoare in *Ancient Wiltshire* where he wrote of 'a cottage adjoining the trackway referred to by the fanciful title of Glory Ann'. The name, which survived on the Ordnance Survey until recent times but has now been dropped, has exercised the minds of antiquarians and etymologists over many years. Speculation about the origin of the 'fanciful' name began with Colt Hoare. Later in the 19th century the Rev. A.C. Smith noted 'The strange name of Glory Ann, which has been a sore puzzle to antiquarians'. Interest continued and early in the present century Edward Thomas referred to the etymological problems raised by the name Glory Ann in his introduction to a reprint of Isaac Taylor's *Words and Places* (1911).

The study of place-names and their origin is recognised to be a notoriously difficult subject fraught with pitfalls. On Greenwood's map of 1820 we find 'Glory Ann or Port Lorien'. 'Port' as a place-name in country districts normally indicates a way to a market, and it seems possible that Glory Ann was the

Wiltshire peasants' corruption of the name Port Lorien, a suggestion which becomes quite feasible when it is remembered that St Anne's Hill above the Vale of Pewsey became corrupted into Tan Hill. But why Port Lorien? The presence of the Knights Templar for some time in the 13th century Temple Farm one mile east of Glory Ann leads to inevitable speculation about Port Lorien being a Templar name.

One of the principal objectives of the Knights Templar was to keep open the ways of pilgrims to the Middle East, then known as the Orient. After being suppressed early in the 14th century the Knights Templar were succeeded by the Knights of St John, also known as the Knights Hospitallers, of which the St John's Ambulance Brigade is a modern survival. When in 1798 this decaying order was expelled by Napoleon from Malta their considerable treasure was loaded aboard the French flagship called *L'Orient*. This Port Lorien-*L'Orient* connection seems to be extremely tenuous, although at least one old history states that Port Lorien was named after the French flagship. It would seem to be far more probable that the name derives from the Orient, meaning the east, for the Knights Templar were active upon Crusades in the Middle East at a time when the Far East was unknown. Nevertheless, both Parish Registers and Census returns in the 19th century sometimes nominate 'L'Orient' as the alternative name for Glory Ann. It may also be relevant to note that the motto of the Knights Templar was the Latin version of the first two lines of Psalm 115: *Non nobis, Domine, non nobis, sed Nomini Tuo da gloriam* (Bestow glory not to us, O Lord, not to us but to Thy Name). Could the last word of this Latin motto have provided Glory Ann with its name?

All that remains on the site today are the two ponds, the smaller being almost dry at most seasons. Sarsen stone, flint, and brick rubble are to be seen about twenty yards north of the ponds. The absence of roofing materials suggests that all the original buildings would have been thatched, and this is confirmed by an old sale catalogue.

In 1723 William Stukeley recorded seeing at Glory Ann a large prehistoric temple and possible mortuary enclosure with standing stones which he called 'Old Chapel', traditions of which may have contributed to the mysterious reputation of this strange place.

The old maps including the first Ordnance Survey show a number of parallel ways diverging from the Ridgeway on Hackpen, passing Glory Ann and running through Totterdown Woods past the former 'Brick Kilns' in the woods and on through Old Totterdown to Marlborough. These ways are now reduced to a single narrow footpath through the dense woods which leaves the Ridgeway through a gate (126729) and follows a hedgeline marked by piles of sarsen stones removed over the years from the fields, finds its way through Totterdown Woods, and upon emerging from the woods (at 138718) forks. The left branch descends gently eastwards among sarsen stones past The Beeches and over Manton Down above Rockley, and continues across Barton Down and Marlborough Common to Marlborough. The right branch provides an alternative way to Marlborough over Clatford Down past Long Tom and along the Kennet Valley.

Stukeley's 1724 drawing of 'Old Chapel' on Hackpen Hill.

Wick Bottom

Wick Bottom is the secluded coombe which runs north-west from Rockley and lies a little north of Temple Bottom. It was formerly known as 'Langdon Wick', and Wick Down to its immediate south was *montum vocatum Wyke* in a 1570 Pembroke Survey. It is within the parish of Preshute. Geoffrey Grigson loved high, dry upland coombes such as Temple and Wick Bottoms, which he described as 'each a green swell of turf rounding up on either side of a central lane'. On the north side of Wick Bottom the towering presence of Rockley Down seems to frown over this little coombe which was shortly after the 1939-1945 the location for the film 'The Scarlet Pimpernel' starring David Niven who had local connections. His first wife Primula came from Wiltshire and is buried at Huish in the Vale of Pewsey.

Wick Bottom was farmed from prehistoric times and in 1194 was granted by Richard I to Stanley Abbey for the rearing of sheep. Man's Head, the knoll immediately north of Wick Bottom (at 140738), is believed to have been the Saxon meeting place of the Preshute Hundred. The modern estate maps of Wick Down Farm designate Man's Head as Deadman's Head.

Stanley Abbey continued to hold Wick Bottom until its Dissolution in 1536 when Langdon Wick was granted to Edward, Viscount Beauchamp the eldest son of Sir John Seymour. The Seymours were descended from a Norman family from St Maur in Normandy. They had come to England in the 13th century and their fortunes were founded upon the Wardenship of Savernake Forest which was obtained by the marriage in 1426 of Roger Seymour to Maud Esturmy, the last of the hereditary Esturmy Wardens of Savernake.

In May 1536 Henry VIII married Sir John Seymour's daughter Lady Jane Seymour. Edward Seymour, Viscount Beauchamp, thus became brother-in-law to the king and was granted extensive estates including Langdon Wick. When Sir John died late in 1536 Edward succeeded him as Warden of Savernake Forest, and when in 1547 Jane Seymour bore the king his longed for son Edward Seymour was created Earl of Hertford. At Henry's death in 1547 his ten year old son succeeded as Edward VI and Hertford became a member of the Regency. In this capacity he demonstrated such ability that he was soon made Lord Protector of the Realm and given the title Duke of Somerset.

Lord Protector Somerset was an acquisitive man who had become immensely rich from lands including the Langdon Wick estate which had been confiscated from the church, but his religious convictions were constant and under his administration moderate Protestantism gained a firm hold in England. He was a brilliant and brave soldier and a just administrator who deplored Henry VIII's terrorist methods and repealed the statute that had made the spoken word treason. Remarkably for the time, during his period of rule no one was either tortured or executed for their religious views. He attempted to restrict the depradations of the rich on the poor and consequently became very popular among the common people but was conspired against by his rivals, particularly by the Duke of Northumberland. Evidence against him was obtained by torture and bribery, and in January 1552 he was executed on a charge of high treason, his estates including Langdon Wick being forfeited to the Crown. When he was executed it is said that people dipped their handkerchiefs in his blood in the belief that he was a martyr, but the young king who had disliked his uncle noted laconically in his diary: 'Somerset had his head cut off'.

At the accession of Queen Mary in 1553 Somerset's estates were restored to his son and Wick remained in the Seymour family until 1779 when it came into the ownership of Charles William Wyndham, son of the Earl of Egremont. It then passed through several hands and became part of the Meux Estate until 1906 when it was sold to George Cowling who died in 1913. The Wick Estate was in 1920 sold to Mr A.J. Hurditch who also acquired Temple Farm and lived at Wick Down Farm for several years.

The Tithe Commissioners in 1846 designated the estate 'Langden Wyke' and although the farm was basically a sheep and corn farm other enterprises were tried here. The 1871 census returns for 'Langden Wick' schedule a horse-training establishment with a trainer, several jockeys, and stablemen and boys. From about 1850 the rich deposits of sarsen stone were being exploited by the Cartwright family of sarsen masons until by 1905 nearly all the sarsens had been broken up and carted away (see *Wiltshire Archaeological Magazine* 63). From 1913-1920 the Stratton family farmed Wick as tenants, and during the Great War the *Marlborough Times* for 19 February 1915 reported the presence at Wick, Temple and Rockley of from two to three hundred injured horses from the front and from Salisbury Plain.

Rockley

Both Temple Bottom and Wick Bottom run south-east down to Rockley, a delightful secluded downland village described by Geoffrey Grigson as offering 'an essence of downland'. Rockley, which is well worth incorporating in walks, is accessible down a cul-de-sac which leaves the Marlborough to Wootton Bassett road two miles north-west of Marlborough near Old Eagle, an intriguing place-name which derives from a former inn which stood beside the turnpike here but was burnt down. The hazards of assuming the obvious in place-names is illustrated by the fact that Rockley does not derive from the sarsen stones from which it is to a great extent built. In Domesday it was

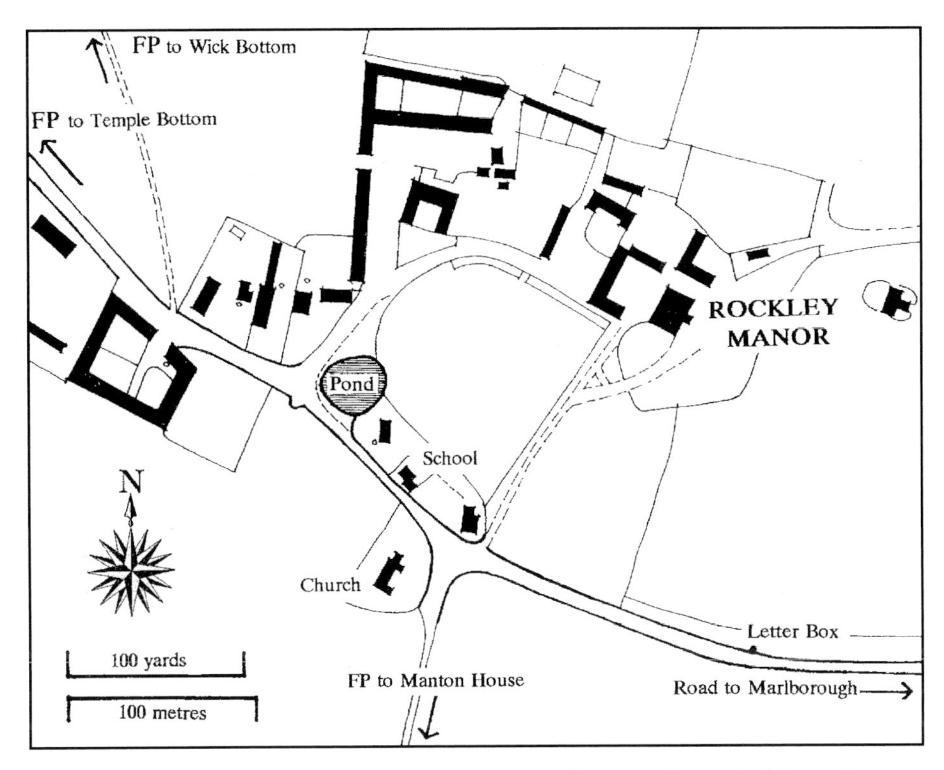

Above: Rockley in 1900; Below: Rockley (in trees in centre) from the Marlborough to Broad Hinton road.

Rochelie, meaning 'rooks' clearing'.

Rockley was essentially an agricultural village and an incident occurred here during the 1830 agricultural riots protesting against the introduction of threshing machinery on the local farms. A young man called Peter Withers was alleged to have injured a magistrate with a hammer and the opportunity was taken to make him an example. The full rigours of the law were applied, and he was sentenced to death, although that sentence was commuted to transportation to Van Diemen's Land – now Tasmania.

In 1855 Rockley and its surrounding land was bought by Mr William H. Tanner who built its tiny school and its church, now both redundant and put to other uses. The present occupants of the early-19th century Rockley Manor are the Millais family who are related to Sir John Everett Millais (1829-1896), the pre-Raphaelite painter who became presisident of the Royal Academy.

An old song called 'In Rockley Firs' was collected locally and was preserved by Alfred Williams in his *Folk Songs of the Upper Thames*.

W.H. Hudson suggested that 'All weathers are good to those who love the open air', and an infinite variety of walks may be obtained by walking these remote uplands at different seasons and in varying weathers. The landscapes of Wiltshire should be experienced at all seasons, for a walk over the same terrain can be an entirely different experience at different seasons and weather conditions and bleak wintry weather positively enhances the atmosphere of these austere uplands. One of my most memorable walks was on a Good Friday over Fyfield Down after a snowy night, when the snow was still lying on the downs and the sarsens and patches of green grass were showing through the slow thaw.

Having stated earlier that I am always utterly at ease in the hospitable landscape of Overton Down and Fyfield Down, by contrast I frequently sense that the Temple and Wick areas possess a stranger atmosphere than any other district that I know in Wiltshire. This may arise from knowledge of the former Templar presence here, the facts that they were a semi-secret society and that when they were suppressed confessions of weird and unnatural practices were extracted from them by barbarous tortures, but I believe that my feelings arise from something more than the Templar presence. William Stukeley's discovery in the 18th century of his 'Old Chapel' mortuary enclosure at Glory Ann may have survived in local lore, and Glory Ann Pond is a mysterious place with a bad reputation. Although I am not of a nervous disposition, I sometimes feel just a little ill-at-ease if I remain at Glory Ann for long alone. Its evil reputation may have arisen merely from the fact that in the last century local youths would hide in the barn that formerly existed at Glory Ann and wave lamps from its interior to frighten people returning after dark from Marlborough Fair. When I wander from Glory Ann over Rough Hill and down past the earthwork remains of the medieval enclosure that I believe may once have been a Templar establishment into Wick Bottom I invariably become extremely conscious of the former presence in this area of the Knights Templar.

Violent and strange happenings have been recorded on these downs. The Wiltshire Coroners' Bill record several deaths and suicides. In July 1754 Elizabeth Rogers was killed on Temple Down, although the four persons accused of her murder were acquitted. Twelve years later a Winterbourne Bassett man was found dead on Temple Down in severe weather. As recently as 1924 a destitute Birmingham man who in his dire need had robbed Winterbourne church wandered into this area and, troubled in his conscience, hanged himself in the copse called The Beeches (147717) leaving an incongruous suicide note which ended: Sorry to give any one trouble, George Thompson. No flowers by request'. Early in the present century the *Marlborough Times* carried several reports of strange happenings at the local farms which led to them being deserted by the families that occupied them.

This is a rather lugubrious note with which to end my description of this area of sensationally beautiful downland, but it is entirely appropriate for in no other part of Wiltshire, other than perhaps on Wansdyke, is the spirit of history felt so strongly and the landscape so utterly pervaded by feelings for its historic past.

Devil's Den in Clatford Bottom

Suggested Walks in the Central Marlborough Downs

2A: Avebury to Fyfield and Overton Downs (about 6 miles allowing 2 miles for wandering east of the Ridgeway; map 173):
If Fyfield Down is approached from Avebury by Green Street (formerly the Old London Way) as it runs east from Avebury the effort of walking up the long gentle gradient from Avebury will be richly rewarded. One and a half miles out of Avebury the way crosses the Ridgeway (125708) on Overton Down and enters the Fyfield Down Nature Reserve. As it continues east of the Ridgeway sarsen stones begin to appear intermittently among the sheep – Grey Wethers among wethers. After a further half a mile over the unhedged downland the Old London Way crosses the shoulder of Overton Down and plunges down the incline known as The Gangway (131709) at the south-west corner of Delling Copse into the head of Clatford Bottom. Here the full splendour of this sarsen littered unimproved (that is unploughed) landscape is suddenly revealed. A day can easily be spent in exploring this fascinating landscape with its sarsen stones and great variety of archaeological sites. The pleasures offered by this area are immense and are all the more enjoyable because they are not too easily obtained, a short walk being necessary in order to experience them.

2B: Rockley to Fyfield and Overton Downs (about 5 miles: map 173):
Fyfield and Overton Downs may alternatively approached by walking west from Rockley village (where cars can be parked among the beeches at the west end of the village) south-west up Lovers' Walk (157717). Another access point to this area is from the small public car park north of the A4 at Manton House.

2C: Hackpen Hill to Fyfield and Overton Downs (about 6 miles: map 173):
Alternatively a car may be left at the car park on the Ridgeway on Hackpen Hill. From here Fyfield and Overton Downs may be reached by a walk south down the Ridgeway for 2.5 miles past Glory Ann, branching left over a stile (127714) north-west of Delling Copse. This route brings the walker to Overton Down at The Gangway (131709) a little west of Fyfield Down.

2D : To Glory Ann from various starting points (distance varies : map 173) :

Glory Ann – one of the most remote places in the Marlborough Downs – may be reached by a 2.5 mile uphill walk (5 miles both ways) north-east from Avebury, by a walk of similar length along Temple Bottom from Rockley, or by a pleasant almost level stroll of 1.5 miles from the road crossing of the Ridgeway on Hackpen Hill above the White Horse, walking south down the Ridgeway and forking left through a gate (126730) where the Ridgeway executes a sharp turn to the right. This walk is well worth the effort of walking the three miles involved as a visit to Glory Ann leads the walker into some of the most glorious downland scenery in Wiltshire, with near at hand the distinctive sarsen rock-strewn landscapes of Fyfield Down and Overton Down. Glory Ann may also be incorporated in walks to Fyfield and Overton Downs by walking from the latter north-west (from 143714 on Clatford Down) through Totterdown Woods.

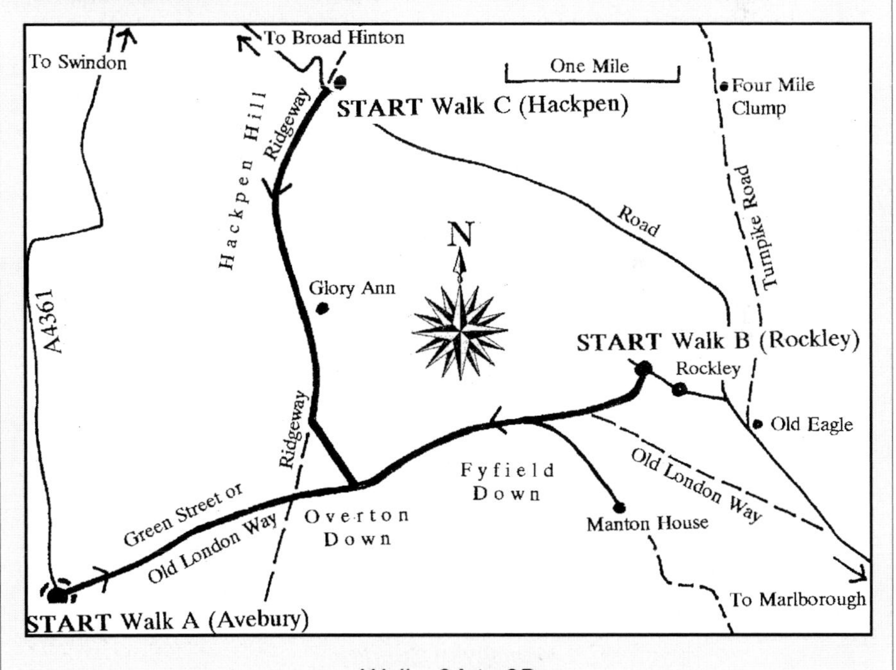

Walks 2A to 2D

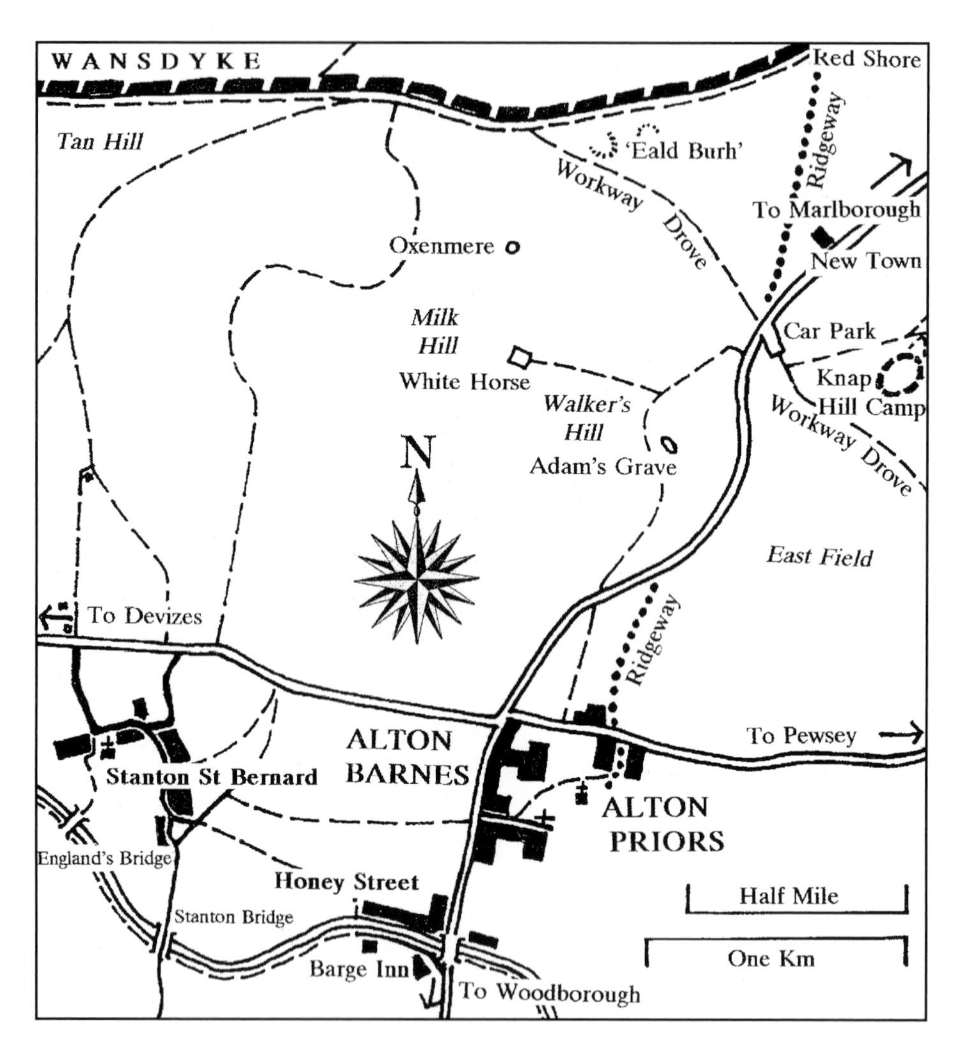

Wansdyke Country

3 Wansdyke

including the Ridgeway across Pewsey Vale, Tan Hill and Shaw

(map Landranger 173)

The Wansdyke countryside is generally, for the purposes of this chapter, defined as the district between the A4 on Overton Hill and the southern escarpment of the Marlborough Downs, although I have ventured south of this area in my investigation of the lost route of the Ridgeway across the Vale of Pewsey.

Although the Countryside Commission's Ridgeway Long Distance Trail ends at Overton Hill (119681) one and a half miles south-east of Avebury, the historic Ridgeway is known to have continued south across the Vale of Pewsey and beyond. The section of the Ridgeway which extends over the Wansdyke countryside south of the Countryside Commission's terminus provides excellent walking, as do the alternative routes by which the Ridgeway may have crossed the Vale of Pewsey and risen up the north escarpment of Salisbury Plain.

The Ridgeway south of Overton Hill

The precise route of the continuation of the Ridgeway south of Overton Hill is known for four miles as it passes through East Kennett village, over Furze Hill through Wansdyke and between the col between Walker's Hill and Knap Hill before descending to Alton Priors, but the route by which it crossed the Vale of Pewsey is now uncertain. The reason for the uncertainty is the geographical problem posed by the Vale and the construction along the valley of the Kennet and Avon Canal in the late 18th century and the railway in 1862 which probably contributed to the obliteration of the route of the Ridgeway.

After having followed the long arc of Hackpen Hill the Ridgeway, as described in Chapter 1, runs due south and reaches Overton Hill where the Countryside Commission's Long Distance Trail ends at the A4. The ancient Ridgeway then continued to run south to cross the River Kennet and pass along the road through East Kennett village east of the tree-covered and unexcavated East Kennett long barrow. It then crosses Wansdyke and passes between Walker's Hill and Knap Hill before descending into the Vale of Pewsey. The Ridgeway then probably commenced its crossing of the valley by passing near the churches of Alton Priors and Alton Barnes. In *The Vale of Pewsey* (1954) H.W. Timperley wrote:

> The Ridgeway, after grooving the slope below the road, is still faintly traceable through Alton Priors, east of the church, and the older One-inch maps of the Ordnance Survey even continue it a short distance beyond the village, cutting it off before it reaches the canal.

The Ridgeway descending from Red Shore in Wansdyke towards the Vale of Pewsey (Knap Hill, left)

The crossing of the Vale of Pewsey occupies a distance of about five miles. Timperley suggested there is always the probability that the Ridgeway divided into several seasonal tracks in crossing the Vale and this was certainly the usual practice of old tracks crossing low-lying ground as travellers cast about in search of better going after the principal way had been pounded to mud and made impassible by traffic ruts. The significant names of Honey Street and Broad Street now occur on its line, significant because the name 'street' in country districts generally indicates the existence of an old road. Honey Street suggests a glutinous surface, just as the name Broad Street indicates a widening of the way.

From the minor road that runs north to south across the valley, at Broad Street a footpath leaves the road on the right (at 106591) and runs a little east of Puckshipton House across former water-meadows to enter the west end of Wilsford village. Part of this route from east of Puckshipton north-east to Gores (106591) was referred to as 'along the road' in a Saxon land charter of 892 AD. This reference suggests that this could be the line of the former Ridgeway, although an alternative line is the continuation of the road southwards to Cuttenham Farm (107571) east of Wilsford. Here the road turns sharply right but a track fords the headwaters of the Salisbury Avon at the ford (107569) south of Cuttenham Farm beside the modern road bridge. The ford was marked *Tealton Forda* in Gothic lettering on the early large-scale Ordnance Maps and *Tiolta's Ford* in a land grant of 892 AD. Wilsford is perhaps significantly the only 'ford' name on this stretch of the river. After Wilsford the two lines run parallel as they mount Wilsford Hill, the Puckshipton route past the Iron Age fortress of Broadbury Banks (093556), the *Tealton Forda* line six hundred yards east of the hillfort along a parish boundary. A road which follows a parish boundary is likely to be a very old road for the coincidence suggests that the road preceded the boundary for which it provided the line. The Puckshipton line is shown with a positive continuation on Andrews and Dury (1773), but the line which crosses the ford near Cuttenham Farm is not continued south from the ford on the 1773 map.

Timperley considered (in *The Vale of Pewsey*) that the Ridgeway 'mounts the scarp of the Plain where the earthworks of Broadbury Banks overlook Wilsford and is back in its own downland world on its way to the south-west by St Joan à Gores and Imber the lost'. In *The Icknield Way* (1913) Edward Thomas, speculating about the route of the Ridgeway beyond Avebury, suggested that it went 'up and over the downs again to the Avon Valley, up to Salisbury Plain and across it, perhaps to the Dorset coast, or skirting it to Warminster and the west'.

At the point on Wilsford Hill where the Ridgeway regains the high ground and possibly changed direction back to the western trend which it has followed since its crossing of the Thames at Streatley, Andrews and Dury on their 1773 map of Wiltshire showed a mound and designated it 'Chalk Ball'. In former times mounds of chalk known as 'chalk lights' were often placed at intervals along traffic routes on Salisbury Plain to guide travellers across the open downs. Ball (or 'Boll') was an early term for hill, and William Stukeley on his drawing of the Avebury district labelled Windmill Hill 'Windmill boll'.

This digression into the route of the Ridgeway across Wansdyke country and its continuation across the Vale of Pewsey has been undertaken because this subject is of some relevence to walkers since an exploration of these routes beyond the recognised Ridgeway can provide much good walking. Practically all of these possible routes of the Ridgeway survive as public rights of way and may be followed in a search for its true line, although the occupation of Salisbury Plain by the military makes exploration further into the Plain impossible. Now I return to the subject of Wansdyke and its asociated countryside.

As it runs south from the A4 at Overton Hill the Ridgeway immediately passes the prehistoric site known as The Sanctuary. This was a circular monument consisting of concentric circles of stones and post holes which, since the West Kennet Avenue links Avebury to The Sanctuary, probably represent the remains of a roofed building which was used for ceremonial purposes. The Sanctuary was originally Neolithic but had an extended history. Its remains were finally dismantled in the 18th century after they had been recorded by William Stukeley and The Sanctuary was rediscovered and excavated in 1930.

The River Kennet

If the known line of the Ridgeway is followed south from the A4 at Overton Hill, a large isolated Bronze Age barrow (119678) is soon passed on the incline down to the River Kennet. On this slope betwen Overton Hill and the River Kennet the Anglo-Saxon levies intercepted a Danish host in 1006 when the Vikings were ravaging England. The Kennet was at one time one of the very finest chalk streams in England, a fisherman's paradise which has been designated a Site of Special Scientific Interest, although in recent years its headwaters regularly dry up in summer and its beauty vanishes as it becomes a dry grass-grown channel.

The low water levels at the head of the River Kennet are attributed by many to the water extraction carried out by the water board from its boreholes at Axford pumping station near Ramsbury. At the time of the Viking invasions the river was probably a considerable obstacle. At any rate the Saxons decided to dispute the crossing of the Kennet at the point where a footbridge now spans the river (119677). The *Anglo-Saxon Chronicle* reads 'Then levies were mustered there at East Kennett, and there they joined battle, but the Danes soon put that force to flight, and bore their plunder to the sea'.

From this Kennet footbridge the Ridgeway continues south, passes to the east of East Kennett along the line of the minor road past the village and then runs on as a trackway over Lurkeley Hill to climb Furze Hill and pass through Wansdyke at Red Shore (118648), so called from the red earth of this area, a 'shore' being a gap – in this case in Wansdyke.

Footbridge at the crossing by the Ridgeway of the River Kennet south of Overton Hill, looking north. On the slope in the background the Anglo-Saxon levies opposed the Danish army in 1006 A.D.

In its progress over Furze Hill before reaching Wansdyke the Ridgeway passes above a litter of sarsen stones in the coombe to its west which was labelled 'Stoneyfield' on the 1773 map by Andrews and Dury. This coombe includes what is believed to have been a prehistoric stone circle (117657) known as Langdean Circle, 'Langdean' meaning Long Dean or valley. It is alternatively known as the Thorn Hill Stone Circle, Thorn Hill being the hill immediately to its west. In *The Archaeology of Wessex* (1958) L.V. Grinsell described this circle as being of 'unusual interest', and mentions 'two roughly parallel rows of sarsens placed upright 10-13 yards apart and some 45 yards long to the east end of the circle'. Unfortunately this site, which lies about three-quarters of a mile south of the unexcavated East Kennet long barrow, is not accessible as there are no public footpaths along the coombe, but it is overlooked from the Ridgeway.

Wansdyke

This stretch of the Ridgeway from Overton Hill to Wansdyke provides good walking and Wansdyke itself offers some of the most dramatic walking in Wiltshire, particularly on the glorious stretch of the dyke from near Walker's Hill to Tan Hill which follows the north escarpment of the Vale of Pewsey at the southern edge of the Marlborough Downs. L.V.Grinsell suggested in *The Archaeology of Wessex* (1958) that 'The walk along the twelve miles or so of Wansdyke between Morgan's Hill and Savernake Forest provides one of the most spectacular experiences in British archaeology'– and such pleasures are not restricted to archaeologists.

The very name of Wansdyke is almost as magical as the countryside around it, being derived from the name *Wodnes dic* which the Saxons gave it. *Woden* – sometimes *Odin* – who gave his name to Wednesday (*Wodnes dag*), was the supreme Norse and Saxon god, the ancestor of their kings, their god of war and the leader of hosts in whose name the Saxon tribes took possession of Britain. The dyke has been proved by excavation to be post-Roman, thrown up to resist forces approaching Pewsey Vale from the north, probably at the time when rival Saxon forces were advancing from the south coast and along the Thames Valley. It blocked the Ridgeway on Furze Hill at the point a little north of the point where the old track crossed the col between Walker's Hill and Knap Hill to cross Pewsey Vale. As a consequence of the strategic importance of this point, two major Saxon battles were fought here, the Battle of Woden's Barrow (*Wodnesbeorg*) in 592 and the Battle of Adam's Grave in 715.

Having been constructed as a defensive earthwork, Wansdyke later became a traffic route followed by drovers bringing their flocks and herds across these inhospitable bleak downs to the great stock fair that was held from early times on Tan Hill. It became a recognised traffic route from medieval times and it remains today a public right-of-way for most of its length.

Despite the fact that in establishing parish boundaries, prominant landscape features were invariably used to define them on the ground, the parish boundaries of this area generally ignore Wansdyke and cross it as though it did not exist, a fact which suggests that Wansdyke post-dates the Anglo-Saxon boundaries. Excavation has confirmed that the dyke is late-Roman or post-Roman, and Saxon land charters suggest that it was probably in existence by 778 AD and definitely by 825. No one can now be certain, but it seems probable that Wansdyke was constructed during the 7th century.

No place in Wiltshire is more redolent than Wansdyke of the immediately post-Roman period known as the Dark Ages to which the construction of

Wansdyke belongs. These uplands crossed by the great dyke create an atmosphere which evokes the remote historic past of Wansdyke and its surrounding countryside. It is perhaps inevitable that stories of strange happenings are associated with the area.

A great deal of folklore has become attached to long barrows which were given evocative names by the Saxons who had no knowledge of their creators. Beside Adam's Grave long barrow – the Saxon *Wodnesbeorg* – on the summit of Walker's Hill a lady once claimed to have been startled by resounding hoofbeats when there were no horses near. She believed that this was an echo of one of the battles fought here in 592 or 715 when the Saxon invaders were contending over Wessex.

On another occasion a group of three shepherds on Tan Hill – and shepherds were regarded as the most sober and reliable members of the rural working community – claimed to have seen and heard a funeral procession proceeding along Wansdyke. A wagon drawn by black horses bearing a coffin was accompanied by men carrying flaming torches. A similar cortège is said to have also been seen on Wansdyke above Huish. It has been suggested that these apparitions were the funeral procession of King Arthur's queen Guinevere, although Amesbury where Guinevere died lies directly east of Glastonbury where she was buried and the points on Wansdyke where these apparitions were seen are fifteen miles north of Amesbury and the expected route to Glastonbury.

Wansdyke on Tan Hill, looking west

Tan Hill

Wansdyke is at its most magnificent on Tan Hill (082647), the joint highest hill in Wiltshire which rises to 964 feet (297m). Here the dyke follows the undulations of the hills that form the south escarpment of the Marlborough Downs and the north escarpment of Pewsey Vale. Its windings and undulations over this stretch emphasise the sinuous character of Wansdyke as it pursues its route above the Vale of Pewsey before descending to New Shepherd's Shore on the A361.

Tan Hill forms part of the dramatic north escarpment of the Vale of Pewsey. Its name is generally assumed to be a corruption by local people of its former name of St Anne's Hill, the name under which it appears on the map of Wiltshire made by Andrews and Dury in 1773, although it is possible that Tan is the older name and that St Anne's was a Christianisation of it.

Fire is an exciting element, and the discovery of how to generate it, with all of its implications for warmth and cooking, must have been a revelation to prehistoric man. The principal of the ever burning flame was practised by many early civilisations including the Egyptian, Greek and Roman, and it survives today in the Olympic flame. Fire festivals were held throughout Europe and especially among the Germanic tribes which colonised England. Consequently there is a strong fire element in many folklores, a modern

The Marlborough Downs from Wansdyke (with Four Mile Clump middle left)

English example being the persistant way in which the tradition of Guy Fawkes fires on bonfire night has survived. It may be significant in the context of Tan Hill that *Tan Hoel* is Celtic for 'Fire of Helios, or of the Sun. J.Thurnam wrote of Tan Hill in the *Wiltshire Archaeological Magazine* (Volume 4) in 1858: 'There can be little doubt that this hill has been the site of Pagan rites far older than Christianity'. In *The Marlborough Country* (1932) H.C. Brentnall suggested that 'the last use of the pagan bonfire was to guide drovers to the spot [Tan Hill] before dawn', for the business of the fair used to begin very early. This practice may well have been a survival from a pagan custom of lighting bonfires which may have been lighted on Tan Hill for some ancient rites connected with a fire festival. In Chapter 1 of this book the possibility of Silbury Hill having been a shrine to the element of water was propounded. Here at Tan Hill, three miles south-west of Silbury, another element, that of fire, may have been worshipped. Now the fires on Tan Hill and its fair have all gone, and we are left to speculate about a name.

Tan Hill Fair

A great stock fair was held at Tan Hill on St Anne's Day (6 August) and the following day from at least the 15th century until 1932. The holding of a fair in such a remote and inaccessible situation suggests a long tradition having existed for such activity on this site. A barn on Tan Hill shown in a drawing made by William Stukeley in the early 18th century was marked by Andrews and Dury (1773) as 'St Ann's Barn' and was shown on Colt Hoare's plate of Wansdyke in his *Ancient Wiltshire* (1819). This barn would presumably have been used for storing the hurdles for the fair, to which came sheep, cattle, and horses. There was also an ancillary pleasure fair on the day following the stock fair. John Aubrey was mistaken when he wrote 'On St Anne's Hill, vulgarly called Tan Hill, every year is kept a great fair within an old camp the commodities are sheep, oxen, and fineries'. The fair was in fact held on the open downs beside Wansdyke, which Aubrey appears to have mistaken for the ramparts of a fortified camp.

Tan Hill Fair provided a great social occasion for people living for many miles around, and from 1825 until its extinction over a hundred years later accounts of Tan Hill fair were carried annually by the *Wiltshire Gazette*. In 1823 this newspaper recorded: 'There was full 20,000 sheep penned. Horned cattle included excellent Devonshires and Scots oxen', and in 1825: 'the coops, standings and rope Fences will be erected on Fri. 5th Aug. next, the day before the fair'. In 1848: 'The show of horses very large. Much business, especially in good cart-horses', and in 1856: 'Two large droves of horses from Wales and Ireland which met customers at £20 and £35 each'. These reports make it very evident that Tan Hill Fair was more than the sheep fair which it is generally assumed to have been. The social elements of the fair was emphasised in 1860: 'The Gypsy tribe always abound at this Fair and offer amusements such as throwing at snuffboxes etc.'

By 1862 the *Wiltshire Gazette* was querying the continuation of the fair at its remote and exposed site :

> We do not know whether the Lady Saint (Anne), in whose honour this fair is said to be held, got tired of the annual revel which has taken place upon her breezy summit for so many centuries, but certain it is that for the last few hours we have received a soaking for our pains, and yesterday brought forth a thunderstorm, and a gale which blew down one of the booths and played havoc among the gingerbread stalls.

An evocative description of the fair is included in Mrs Ida Gandy's history of Bishop's Cannings entitled *Round About the Little Steeple* (1960):

> Tan Hill Fair was famous for miles around, and for at least 500 years, and probably a good deal longer, it was a great event in the lives of country people. By a Charter dated Nov. 5, 1499, the Abbess of St Mary's, Winchester, was granted a yearly fair in the parish of All Cannings 'in a place called Charlborough Down by Wansdyke on the feast and morrow of St Anne' (Cal. Charter Rolls, 1427-1516, p273) As they gained the top of the ridge they [the people of Bishop's Cannings] would see, as did people of a later day, flocks of sheep making for Tan Hill from the north, east and west, across the sea of downs, or climbing up from Pewsey Vale. The same clouds of white dust would rise from thousands of small hooves, the same musical clamour of sheep-bells and shouts of shepherds fills the air. Many of these latter had been on the move since the first streak of daylight. They came from perhaps twenty, thirty, or forty miles away and rested through the night with their flocks at some downland farm; or lay in a sheltered hollow or the lee of a clump of trees.
>
> As for the sheep themselves they were the old horned Wiltshire sheep till Southdowns and Hampshire Downs superseded them. Nor was it only sheep that gathered from all points of the compass on Tan Hill. People knew how to walk in those days, and the Fair drew them from near and far.

Beside Wansdyke, above Stanton St Bernard, was kept – and it may still be there for all I know although I have not seen it for a few years – a flock of of the old Wiltshire Horn breed of sheep which was formerly universal in Wiltshire. In this breed the rams, the ewes, and the lambs from a fairly early age were horned. This ancient breed died out in Wiltshire during the 19th century when sheep breeds were undergoing rapid improvement by cross-breeding, but it was reintroduced from a flock that survived outside the county.

Over many centuries drovers drove their herds and flocks to Tan Hill Fair, using Wansdyke to guide them to the fair site. In 1637 Tan Hill Fair was suspended because the plague was raging in Devizes, but it was the superseding of droving animals on the hoof by the use of cattle lorries which finally killed the fair. On 6 August 1932 there was very heavy rain and the lorries got bogged down and could not get on to the hill. They never tried again, although for seven years until the outbreak of war in 1939 the fair continued to be held at an alternative site in the Kennet Valley in a field between Silbury Hill and Swallowhead Springs three miles to the north of Tan Hill.

Early in 1645 an event occurred on Tan Hill during the Civil War. Some time before the Battle of Naseby (June 1645) effectively decided the Civil War in favour of Parliament, Lord Goring, the Royalist commander in the west, was ordered by King Charles to bring his western cavalry to the royal headquarters at Oxford. Prince Rupert, out of jealousy at Goring's influence with the king, managed to get the order rescinded. According to the Earl of Clarendon, the royalist historian, Prince Rupert did not want Goring to come north because he hated him 'as a man of ready wit, and an exceptional speaker' who would have undue influence with the king. Lord Goring, who liked independent command, was quite happy to return to his former sphere of operations around Taunton where he had gained a reputation for ruthlessness. The king then had one of his many changes of mind and in late April, Lord Goring was once again ordered to bring his army to a rendezvous with the king's army at Market Harborough in the Midlands. Goring nominated Tan Hill as the gathering point for his Western Army. Waylen records in his *History Military and Municipal of the Town of Marlborough*:

> Previous to Naseby fight, Lord Goring having been summoned out of the West to join the royal standard, and to gather on his way such troops as he had left in Wilts, came through Devizes on the 1st of May, and appointed the conspicuous eminence of Tan Hill as a rendezvous. His numbers swelled to 3,000, with whom he marched during the following night to a spot called 'Marlborough Thorns'.

Having commenced his ride north-east along Wansdyke towards Marlborough, Goring hesitated in his move to join the main royal army. It is not clear whether he disobeyed orders, or whether his orders were changed. C.V.Wedgwood in *The King's War* (1958) suggests the former, but Colonel H.C.B. Rogers in *Battles and Generals of the Civil Wars* (1968) says that his orders to go north were countermanded. At any event, he did not go. Goring was only too glad to remain in the south, and lingered around Newbury, sending a letter to the king indicating that he was not coming. This letter was intercepted by General Fairfax who seized the opportunity to bring the main royal army to battle at Naseby in an action which effectively decided the war in favour of Parliament, largely as a result of the royalist inferiority in cavalry. It is interesting to speculate whether Goring's presence with the Western Army at Naseby would have affected the outcome of the battle and of the Civil War, and altered the course of history.

Oxenmere on Milk Hill

Above the Alton White Horse is Oxenmere (106642), a hilltop pond situated very near the highest point in Wiltshire. Oxenmere is over a thousand years old, having been mentioned as *Oxnamere* in an Anglo-Saxon charter dated 825. No doubt this pond, a mile and a half west of Tan Hill, was used to water herds and flocks as they neared the fair site. Above Oxenmere and in the fork between Wansdyke and the Workway Drove lies the ancient earthwork known to the Saxons as *Eald Burh* ('Old Town': at 110645), and around Gopher Wood on Draycot Hill are the earthworks of the *boscus de Hulwerk* of the Forest of Savernake Charters, an embanked settlement which may have been the forerunner of the deserted medieval village of Shaw to its north-west.

Shaw Deserted Village

Beside the one mile section of Wansdyke that is no longer a public right of way east of the road from Lockeridge to Alton Barnes, stands Shaw House (131654).

Near Shaw House a village of presumably Saxon origin – for Shaw is a Saxon word – existed at Shaw (136651). The village is mentioned in Domesday but little is known about its history for a number of reasons. In the first place it is remote from all roads and until recently access was difficult, but a 'permissive' path has now been opened to the site by agreement with the landowner. When he excavated the church at Shaw in 1929 Mr H.C. Brentnall of Marlborough College remarked in his report on the 'remote field' in which it was situated. His excavation reports appeared in the *Journal of The Marlborough College Natural History Society* (No. 78: 1929) and in the *Wiltshire Archaeological Magazine* for 1932. In addition to its extreme isolation, the second complication about Shaw is the fact that the parish boundary between Alton Barnes and West Overton passes through the village site. This explains historical references to 'Shaw-in-Alton' and 'Shaw-in Overton'. A third reason which explains our lack of knowledge about Shaw is the apparent complete absence of records. Brentnall recorded that, having made searches at the Public Record Office, the British Museum, at Salisbury, and at Winchester, he had come to the conclusion that Shaw seemed to have no history.

Shaw in fact appears in records defining the limits of jurisdiction of the Forest of Savernake. The word 'shaw' means a small wood or thicket, and in Wiltshire was often used for a narrow strip of woodland. It is from the Old English *scaga*, and Shaw went through the following variations: *Schaga* in 1165, *Saghe* in 1229, *Schages* in 1242, *Shagh* in 1279, and *Shawe* in 1316. Some of these were applied to nearby Shaw House (or Farm). In 1332 fifteenth' and tenth' taxes totalling 6s.5d. (32p) were paid at *Shawe* by John le Kynge, Christine Nyw, William in le Wedere, William Stel, and Roger le W.

Shaw Church was discovered as a result of Mr Frederick Stratton of Shaw House telling Mr Brentnall of the tradition that one of his fields was the site of a former church and, as he believed, of a Saxon settlement. The local tradition had probably been sustained by a 19th century endowment of Alton Barnes Church where we find: 'On Alton Priors Down. No 20a. Churchyard Shaw. Pasture. 1 rood, 15 poles'.

Brentnall's excavations, on which he employed boys from Marlborough College, established the site and form of the church. It was situated about a hundred and twenty yards west of Shaw Copse (at 13836510). The plan

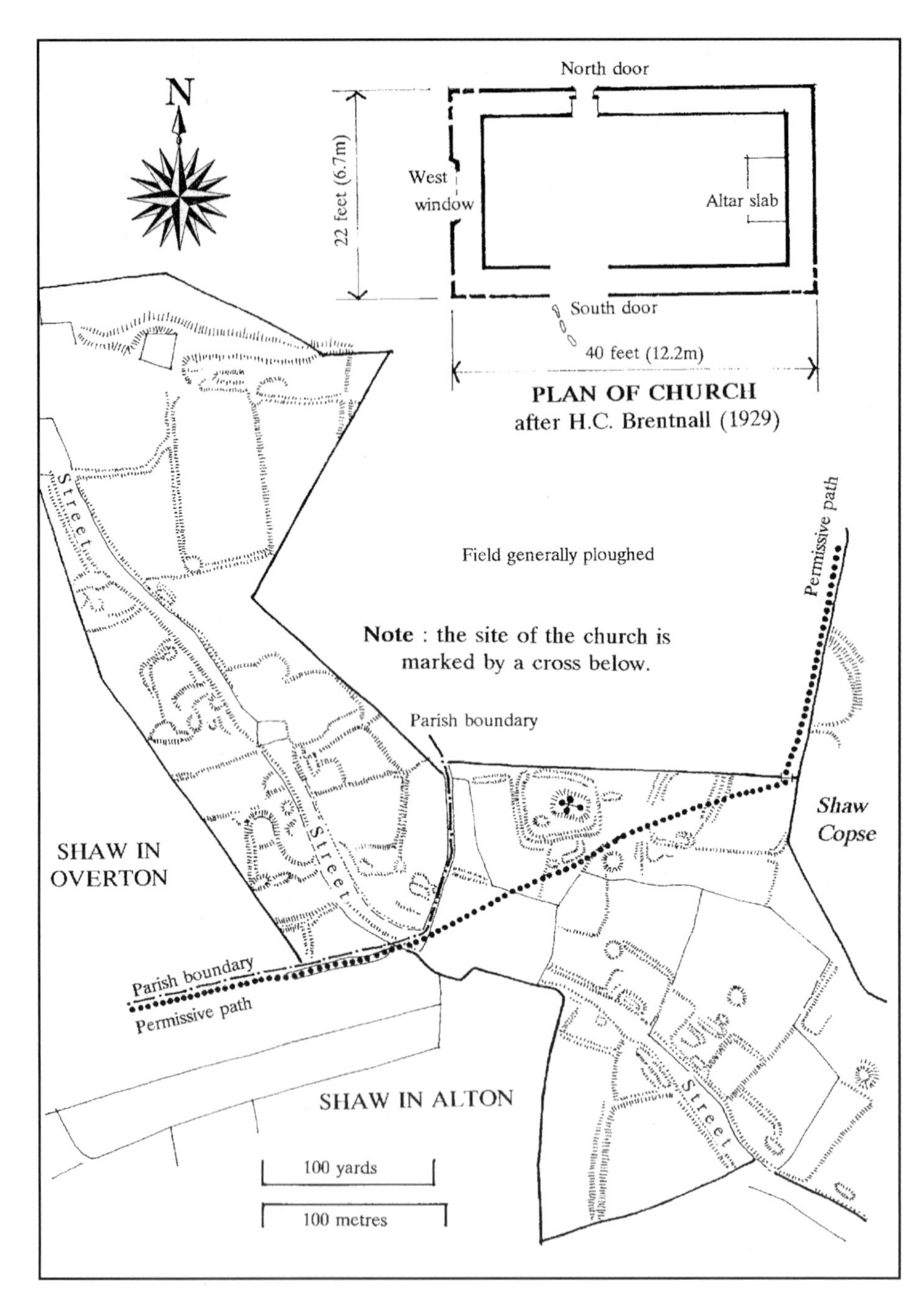

Plan of Shaw deserted village

produced by Brentnall is of a simple rectangular church; outside dimensions about 40 feet by 22 feet (12.2m by 6.7m), internal 36 by 16 feet (11m by 4.9m). The seating area of about 25 feet by 16 feet (7.6m by 4.9m) would comfortably have seated about 50 persons, although at that time the congregation would have remained standing. The extremely simple one-cell plan form with no differentiation between the sanctuary and the nave, together with the apparent lack of buttresses, suggests an early and perhaps an Anglo-Saxon date. Brentnall suggested from finds that the church dated from the early 14th century, but the style of the only window found is Early English and therefore probably 13th century, and this window may have been an insertion into a much earlier church.

Tradition asserted that other buildings including a smithy were associated with the church and the many earthworks which remain visible on the ground indicate an extensive village with a sunken street. It is likely that more buildings existed in the now (1996) ploughed field to the north of the church. This suggestion is supported by the fact that the plan held by Wiltshire County Council archaeologists shows earthworks stopping abruptly at the edge of this ploughed field, and by the fact that the church had a north door which would have been unlikely if all the village extended south and west of the church. The sunken village street was presumably continuous, although at some time it has been filled where the 'permissive' path crosses it. During his excavation Brentnall dug trenches across the churchyard but found no burials. He had neither time nor resources to excavate the village.

Former street at deserted village of Shaw

The geology of the site of Shaw is a capping of clay-with-flints overlying the chalk, which explains the many trees which obscure the aerial photographs of the area which are held by Wiltshire County Council's Library and Museums Service (Archaeological Section). The reason for the existence of Shaw in this remote position should be examined. If Shaw was a Saxon village its proximity to Wansdyke may be significant for it suggests that it may have been a garrison village. Wansdyke has been proved to be post-Roman. It was probably constructed as a defensive frontier by the West Saxons after the Battle of *Deorham* (Dyrham in Avon) in 577 AD. If so it soon failed for in 592 the Battle of *Wodnesbeorg* was fought at Adam's Grave on Walker's Hill, south of Wansdyke and two miles south-west from Shaw village. We have seen that Wansdyke was *Woden's Dyke* and Adam's Grave was *Wodnesbeorg* to the Anglo-Saxons. The *Anglo-Saxon Chronicle* recorded '592 There was a great slaughter in Britain this year at *Wodnesbeorg* and Ceawlin was expelled'. Ceawlin, the king of the West Saxons (of Wessex), was here at Adam's Grave defeated by Ceol.

The date for the desertion of Shaw has never been established. In 1377 the Poll Tax returned only three persons at Shaw, the lowest return in Wiltshire. This probably represented a population allowing for exempted children and the widespread evasion of this unpopular tax of about ten. Such a low return may be a reflection of the effects of the Black Death mortality in 1349 and its subsequent outbreaks later in the 14th century. It is possible that Shaw later revived. Shaw is an upland village at over 750 feet (229m), remote from water. It probably depended upon sheep husbandry and its final desertion may have occurred in the early 15th century when many upland villages were depopulated to make way for more sheep.

The flora of the Wansdyke countryside is immensely rich. Golden Ball Hill is alleged to take its name from the yellow rock-rose *Helianthemum chamaecistus* which is said to have formerly grown here in such profusion that it coloured the hill, although the hill could equally well derive its name from the many cowslips that sprinkle its slopes earlier in the year or from the bird's foot trefoil which grows later in the season on the hill. Towards the end of summer Golden Ball Hill is tinged bronze by the flower heads of the salad burnet which also embellishes the banks of Wansdyke. Walker's Hill and Knap Hill are in spring also covered with milkwort ranging in colour from white to a rich dark blue. The substantial banks of Wansdyke also grow a great variety of wild flowers, for it is characteristic of ancient earthworks on the Wiltshire downlands that being well drained and never ploughed they sustain a flora richer even than that of the adjoining downlands. This applies even to the anthills that occur in the unploughed downland. The rich Wansdyke flora attracts a great variety and profusion of butterflies. At midsummer 1996 I saw on Wansdyke – immediately west of Red Shore (118648) – multitudes of mixed butterflies in which mainly marbled whites and browns predominated, often several to each scabious bloom. Later in the year at precisely the same place there were even greater clouds of butterflies, on this occasion mainly small blues.

Wansdyke should be experienced in all weathers and at all seasons, in bleak as well as in benign weather. To walk Wansdyke – or indeed many other parts of upland Wiltshire – in fierce weather is an exhilarating experience that should not be missed. Fierce winds and pelting rain help to conjure up the atmosphere of its turbulent past in the Dark Ages when this part of Britain was being fiercely disputed between its British post-Roman residents and the invading armies of Saxons. The latter ultimately conquered and settled this area and turned it into Wessex (the kingdom of the West Saxons), and the entire country into England, the land of the Germanic tribe of Angles.

In reflecting on the walking in this countryside around Wansdyke I can say without a moment's hesitation that it provides in my estimation some of the best walking in Wiltshire – arguably the very best – and I earnestly exhort my readers to make every effort to walk the Wansdyke countryside above Pewsey Vale.

Walker's Hill from the Workway Drove. The terracettes are the result of natural erosion of topsoil on a steep chalk slope.

Suggested Walks in Wansdyke Country

The walks available in the Wansdyke countryside are almost unlimited and the sensational nature of the walking along the dyke from Shepherd's Shore to Milk Hill has already been described (page 84). When walking Wansdyke east from New Shepherd's Shore the A361 is best avoided, both for its traffic and for its lack of adequate parking. It is better to go to Bourton at the north end of Bishops Cannings and walk north-east to Wansdyke over Roughridge Hill.

3A: Bourton to Wansdyke (6 miles: map 173): A 6 mile round walk may be taken from Bourton north-east to Wansdyke, east along the dyke to Tan Hill, south to Allington, and then returning west along the Harepath past Easton Farm back to Bourton.

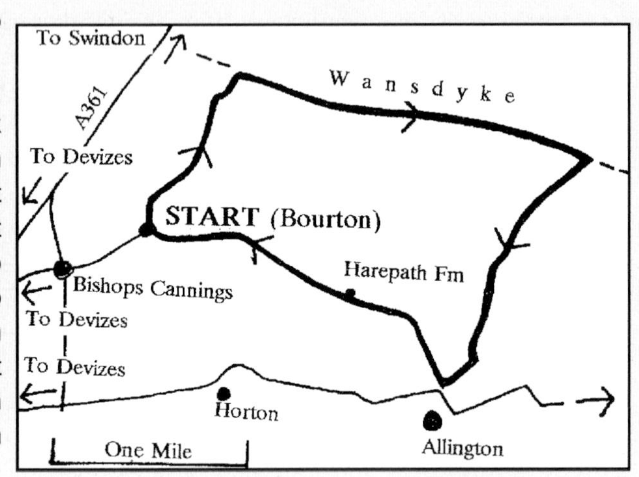

Wansdyke may also be approached from Pewsey Vale to its south (as described later in Chapter 6 on the Vale of Pewsey) but my personal preference is to approach the dyke from the north and come suddenly upon the unexpected great expansive views across the Vale to Salisbury spire 21 miles distant. One of the approaches from the north, along the Ridgeway from Overton Hill, has been described earlier in this chapter (pages 79-82).

3B: East Kennett to Wansdyke (6 or 8 mile options: map 173): An alternative shorter approach to Wansdyke from the north is from East Kennett, walking west past the church, turning south at 113674 and walking over Thorn Hill to Wansdyke east of Tan Hill. The dyke can then be followed west over Tan Hill, the return to East Kennett being north-east from 083651

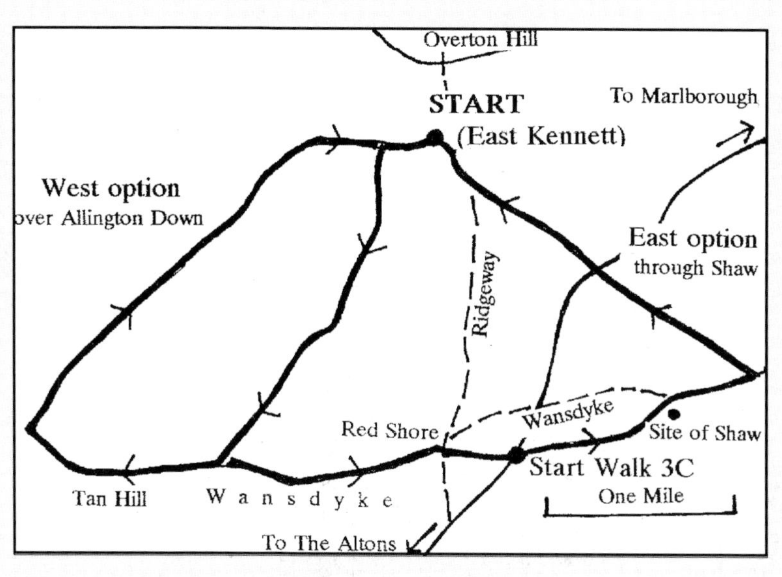

Walks 3B and 3C

over Allington Down (6 miles). An alternative route is to from Tan Hill follow Wansdyke east to Red Shore (118648) and then descend the 'permissive' path east from 117647 across the Lockeridge to Alton Priors road and visit the site of Shaw village. The return may then be into West Woods and north-west down the droveway (through 137659) – note the way that this track is aligned on Silbury Hill straight ahead-and the minor road to East Kennett. (This alternative extends the walk to about 8 miles). It should be emphasised that the stretch of Wansdyke past Shaw House (131654) is not a public right of way.

3C: To Shaw from the Lockeridge to Alton Barnes road (2.5 miles: map 173; see map above):
Access to Shaw deserted village site is easiest from the minor road to its west from Alton Barnes to Lockeridge along the line just described. From 124647 on the Lockeridge to Alton road (where a car may be parked beside a gate) the public footpath running east is followed to 134648. From this point a 'permissive' path over a stile runs north-east to Shaw. Permission to depart from this path should be obtained from the owner of the site at Shaw House.

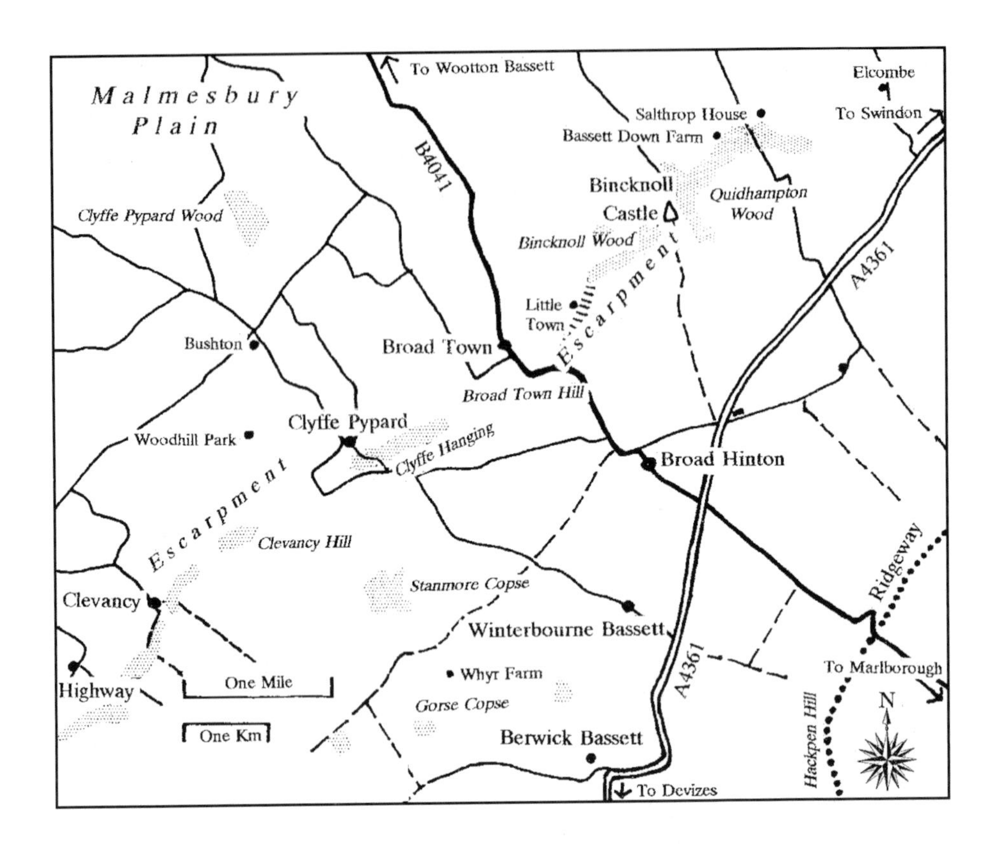

Grigson Country

4 Grigson Country

The lower escarpment of the Marlborough Downs through Highway, Clyffe Pypard and Bincknoll

(map Landranger 173)

Most of the walkers following the Ridgeway along Hackpen Hill as it runs along the western rim of the Marlborough Downs are unaware that this downland escarpment is echoed a few miles to its north-west by an outer escarpment which forms a secondary step separating the chalk uplands from the lower dairying country – the 'cheese' country – which extends from the Wootton Bassett area towards Malmesbury. The extreme contrasts between the chalk downland and the clay plains of the adjoining countryside led to the expression 'as different as chalk and cheese' which is believed to have originated in this area.

This secondary escarpment of the Marlborough Downs, which extends from Highway near Compton Bassett to Bincknoll (pronounce 'By-noll') west of Wroughton, drops about 250 to 300 feet (76m to 91m) from the chalk highland plateau to the extensive plains situated to its north-west which extend from the stony hills of the Cotswolds to the foot of the chalk hills of the Marlborough Downs. Through this vast fertile plain around Malmesbury run several streams, those north and east of Wootton Bassett tending to feed the River Thames while those to its south and west contribute their waters to the Bristol Avon which describes a long curve through this area from its sources near Malmesbury past Chippenham to the Bristol Channel.

The area which is described in this chapter is restricted to the secondary escarpment of the Marlborough Downs which rises from the eastern edge of the Malmesbury Plain and extends from Highway to a little beyond Bincknoll. It provides excellent walking of a quality comparable to that which is offered by the Ridgeway which runs parallel to it and a few miles to its south-east (described in Chapter 1), and the walking here is far more secluded. This escarpment and its associated landscape I have chosen to designate Grigson Country out of deference to the writer and critic Geoffrey Grigson who chose to live here for the latter part of his life from 1946 until his death in the 1985. He loved this countryside and is the only writer to have taken positive notice of it. For me Grigson is inevitably associated with this little-known but particularly attractive part of Wiltshire.

The escarpment runs in an almost straight six mile line from near Highway to Bincknoll Castle two miles north-east of Broad Town. For walking purposes it divides itself naturally into two equal sections either side of Clyffe Pypard which provides a good access point. The southern section extends for three miles south-west to Highway, the other the same distance north-east to Bincknoll. My descripton of the escarpment and its associated landscapes will commence at Highway and progress north-east past Clyffe Pypard to Bincknoll.

The Escarpment from Highway to Clyffe Pypard

The name Highway suggests a through road in an area which is now conspicuously remote from major roads. Two miles to the east of Highway ran an 18th century way known as the 'Vize Way' which was recorded as *Viseweia* in the 13th century, 'Vize' being the old name for Devizes. Its course was from Wroughton south-west past Weir Farm through Broad Hinton and parallel to the escarpment (through 065733) east of Highway on its way through Yatesbury to Devizes.

Small villages usually develop into large ones as a result of good communications. Clyffe Pypard, for example, has remained small as a consequence of being remote from a main road, but Broad Hinton has by contrast grown into a large village as a result of being situated on the main Wootton Bassett to Marlborough road. In the 1332 tax returns Highway paid more than Clyffe Pypard and almost as much as Broad Town. It must later have become insignificant as a result of its highway becoming disused.

From Highway and Clevancy a number of parallel ways which ran south-east survive as public rights of way. The Tithe Map reveals the names Middle Drove (from 051746), and Long Drove or Bourne Drove across Clevancy Field (from 053751). The names indicate that these were at one time cattle droves, and Middle Drove implies that the way to its south over Highway Hill (047743) was also used as a droveway. The fact that in the late-19th century a local labourer told the Rev. A.C. Smith (1822-1898), the vicar of Yatesbury and the secretary of Wiltshire Archaeological Society, that this lane was formerly known as 'The Marlborough Road' suggests that it may once have been an important through way. The former existence of these old traffic routes may explain the name Highway.

Between Highway and Clevancy the steep escarpment along Highway

Geoffrey Grigson

Geoffrey Grigson (1905-1985) was successively a schoolmaster, journalist, publisher, and a radio producer for the BBC. Ultimately he became self-employed as a critic and as the author of much poetry and many books. He was the youngest of seven brothers, five of whom were killed in the two World Wars. Grigson became nationally recognised as both writer and severe critic – severe in that his frank and uncompromising judgements sometimes upset his friends. He wrote a great deal on the countryside in general and on Wiltshire in particular.

Of his Wiltshire writings his many articles in *Country Life* and the little book of photographs with short texts entitled *The Wiltshire Book* (1957) are of particular interest. His more general books, which include *The Shell Country Book* (1962) and *The Shell Country Alphabet* (1966), reveal his profound knowledge of rural England. He also wrote poetry, and books, essays, articles and reviews on many subjects including art and literary criticism, and was in the 1930s the editor of the influential *New Verse*. Geoffrey Grigson was also the author of *The Englishman's Flora* (1958) and the *Dictionary of English Plant Names* (1974). His third wife was the cookery writer Jane Grigson who died in 1990.

In 1936 Grigson bought a cottage in this district at Little Town, east of Broad Town, and from 1946 until the end of his life he lived in Broad Town Farm, the house with the pillared porch at the road junction in Broad Town under Broad Town Hill.

Broad Town Farm, Grigson's home for the latter part of his life.

Hill is wooded. Buzzards are regularly seen and heard around the wooded sections of this escarpment, snipe flight across its wet meadows, and hobbies are occasionally seen. The fine name of Clevancy derives from 'cliff' and the name of its early owner Robert de Wancy who held the manor in the early 13th century, although Cliffansty House (052752) is a fanciful name invented by a late owner.

Deserted Villages at Bupton and Woodhill

The succeeding two mile stretch of the hill between between Clevancy and Clyffe Pypard passes above two deserted medieval village sites situated below the spring line. The site of Bupton village (057761) is under the escarpment and is crossed by several public footpaths. The more extensive earthworks of Woodhill village (060770), which include a substantial Norman moated site, stand beside a stream almost a mile back from the escarpment and a little north of a mound which formerly accommodated a windmill.

Woodhill may be approached by a rather obscure footpath which diverges from the foot of the escarpment (from 060759) and runs north past Bupton and across the site of Woodhill village. Woodhill was formerly *Odehill* and the Woodhill Park name applied to it by the Ordnance Survey commemorates an early medieval deer park which was recorded in documents of 1304 as *Wodhull*, a park owned by Edward de Besylles (or Besils). The 1583 *Note of Parks in the County of Wilts* lists 'Odehill Park' as having a perimeter of one mile and being then in the ownership of Sir Thomas Wroughton. A bank and ditch which is still visible on the ground and runs parallel to the escarpment (063762 to 066764 and shown on the old one-inch and 2.5-inch maps but omitted from more recent maps) is almost certainly a survival of the former banked and ditched perimeter pale of Woodhill Park.

The village of Woodhill, which in Domesday was owned by Odo, Bishop of Bayeux (c1036-1097), the powerful half-brother of William I, may have been depopulated to make way for the deer park. Odo was both a Norman prelate and an English earl. He was the patron who ordered the Bayeux tapestry, and was a brilliant man of the world who during William's absence in Normandy became in 1067, jointly with William FitzOsbern, regent of England. Odo became Earl of Kent, but was expelled in 1088 for conspiring against William Rufus and went to Normandy. When he died at Palermo on the First Crusade, Odo was pressing his claim to become pope.

The fields beneath the escarpment are waterlogged from the many springs which emerge from the spring line, so much so that water-loving trees such as alder grow here grow as isolated specimens in the middle of fields. Many ditches, some of which soon become small streams, run from the spring line north-east towards Wootton Bassett, and there are several ponds, most of them too insignificant to be marked on the map. An indication of the waterlogged nature of the ground below the escarpment is given by the facts that the area below Woodhill was known as 'Marshes', a well-regarded pasture in Broad Town was named 'la lake', by the description which Geoffrey Grigson wrote in his *Recollections* (1984):

> Rather desolate fields without or with only a few paths stretched away from the farm-house I bought in Wiltshire at the end of the war. Curlew flighted from an escarpment into these damp fields, the damp meadows of long coarse grass, saying *curlu, curlu*, as if it were Yorkshire and not Wiltshire.

Clyffe Pypard Village

Clyffe Pypard is a delightful diffuse village containing a fine group of church, manor house, and small lake. A.G. Bradley – correctly in my estimation – described Clyffe Pypard in *Round About Wiltshire* (1907) as 'the most picturesquely seated village in North Wilts'. Its attractive name derives from 'cliff' which is self-explanatory, and 'Pypard' from Richard Pipart or Pipard who owned the manor in 1231. A 1304 charter granted Free Warren – that is the right to take small game – at 'Pipard's Cliffe' to Roger de Cobham. The effigy in the tomb recess in the church may be him.

The manor house beside the lake at Clyffe Pypard was the home of Canon E.H. Goddard, the enthusiastic Wiltshire historian who compiled the invaluable *Wiltshire Bibliography* in 1929 and was for a long time the secretary of the Wiltshire Archaeological Society. Another member of the Goddard family recorded in the *Wiltshire Archaeological Magazine* (Volume 44) that 'There is no stone in the parish [Clyffe Pypard] except the chalk, which when used for building will only endure on the north side of walls'. This chalk block – known in Wiltshire as 'clunch' – probably came from the large circular quarry pit which still exists short distance south of Clyffe Pypard beside the minor road (at 067765). The fact that the flat floor of this quarry, which is approached by a very distinct hollow way running up from Woodhill Park, is now grass-grown indicates that it has been long disused.

Whilst on the subject of quarrying, one of the strongest impressions gained from walking under this escarpment is the way in which, almost throughout its length, the ground has been disturbed by the activities of man in excavating chalk and lime from the scarp foot. This, together with the abandoned villages situated below the spring line of the escarpment, indicates that at some time in the past a considerable population lived here, though

Sir Nikolaus Pevsner

In any densely populated country such as England buildings are inevitably a significant element in the countryside and anyone who professes an interest in landscape should be interested in the buildings which feature in the landscape. The mammoth task of listing, describing and evaluating all of the buildings of any historic value in England was undertaken over a period of many years by the eminent continental art and architecture historian Sir Nikolaus Pevsner (1901-1983) who published his researches in the invaluable The Buildings of England series of county books published by Penguin Books. *The Buildings of England: Wiltshire* appeared in 1963 and has been subsequently updated.

Pevsner and his wife Lola, who predeceased him, are buried at the east end of the churchyard at Clyffe Pypard, their grave being marked by a segmental-headed slate headstone to the left (north) of the path. They are also commemorated by the gates to Clyffe Pypard churchyard which bear brass plates lettered 'LP' and 'NP'.

In the 1930s Nikolaus Pevsner was obliged to flee Hitler's Germany because he was Jewish. Germany's loss proved to be England's gain because, after being interned as an alien, Pevsner after the war commenced his life's work of researching and writing *The Buildings of England.* He was such an ardent scholar, and the travelling involved so endless, that his favourite meal was spaghetti – because it could be eaten rapidly!

The burial of the Pevsners in the remote Wiltshire village of Clyffe Pypard is explained by the fact that Pevsner had been a neighbour of Geoffrey Grigson in London, and when Grigson vacated his cottage (097782) beside Little Town Farmhouse at Little Town (under the White Horse on Snow Hill a little north-east of Broad Town), Pevsner took on the cottage as a study-retreat. Grigson later described this cottage, which he acquired for forty pounds a little before the Second World War broke out, in *The Crest on the Silver* (1950) as 'a minute three-roomed house in ruins under an inland cliff in Wiltshire'. Pevsner's *Wiltshire* volume (1963) of *The Buildings of England* is dedicated 'To Nicholas and Paul, this volume on the county of the cottage'. The house had an outside toilet which Grigson had sited in consultation with the sculptor Henry Moore to take advantage of the fine view from the garden.

Grigson placed on record the following story about his friend. A local villager once spotted the exeptionally thin scholarly and bespectacled figure of Pevsner attempting particularly inneffectually to dig a cess-pit in his garden. The robust Wiltshire villager watched for a short time unbelieving and then, unable to stand such feeble efforts any longer, thrust his way through the hedge crying: 'Let oi do it Doctor Pevsner, let oi do it'.

Grigson once advised his readers: 'Don't stay at home, but go and explore. Don't stay indoors, but go and look! Such an exhortation is equally applicable to the readers of this book.

Pevsner's grave (bottom right) at Clyffe Pypard.

these people must have departed long ago as the villages were not shown by Andrews and Dury on their 1773 map of Wiltshire.

This activity may be a reflection of the time in the 13th century when vast estates in this area were held by the great Norman family of Basset, a fact which explains the suffix names to Wootton Bassett, Compton Bassett, Berwick Bassett, and Winterbourne Bassett. The Bassets provided several Justiciars of England, Justiciars being the chief officers of State under the Norman and Plantegenet kings. Alan Basset (died 1232) owned Wootton Bassett by 1212. He was favoured by both Richard I and King John, and his name appeared as one of the king's counsellors in Magna Carta. Philip Basset (died 1271) became Justiciar in 1261 and was in 1262 left in charge of England when Henry II was away in France. His daughter married Hugh le Despenser who replaced Philip Basset as Justiciar in 1263 and later became the notorious favourite of Edward II. He inherited through his wife the vast Basset estates which he greatly expanded, but his autocratic and grasping behaviour antagonised the Barons of England who went to war with the Despensers, father and son, captured, and summarily executed them.

Canon Goddard's predecessor as vicar of Clyffe Pypard for most of the 19th century rejoiced in the ultra-patriotic name of Horatio Nelson Goddard (1806-1900). He had as a young justice of the peace been active in dealing with rioters during the agricultural riots of 1830.

Clyffe Pypard is a good starting point for walks in either direction along this escarpment. Parking is not possible near the church, but there are wide grass verges available south-west of the village near the site of a former quarry (at about 070766).

The Escarpment from Clyffe Pypard to Bincknoll

A delightful field path leaves Clyffe Pypard churchyard, passes the lake, and runs east (through 078769) under the scarp towards Bincknoll. After a couple of miles it reaches Broad Town where Geoffrey Grigson's house Broad Town Farm stands at the crossroads. Its chimney is carved with the inscription: 'R S 1668'. Upon checking his deeds Grigson discovered that the initials were those of a Richard Spackman. An elaborate eighteen feet high monument to a local carpenter called Thomas Spackman who died in 1786 is a feature of Clyffe Pypard church, and it is evident that the Spackmans – the name is believed to mean spokesman – were a family of local builders. When Geoffrey Grigson extended Broad Town Farm the local builder who built the extension was another Richard Spackman.

A little north-east of Broad Town is its satellite Little Town with Pevsner's cottage situated beside Little Town Farmhouse near the White Horse (098782) which was cut in 1864 by Mr William Saunders of Little Town Farm. Grigson described the view north-west from this cottage at Little Town: 'Looking over this world is like looking over a painting by Koninck [a 17th century painter of panoramic Dutch landscapes] or over the large landscape by Rubens in the National Gallery [the Chateau de Steen, his country house near Antwerp]'. Having lived for two years near Antwerp, and become familiar with its flat landscapes, I can vouch for the fact that the landscape west of this escarpment does indeed bear a marked resemblence to the Flemish landscape.

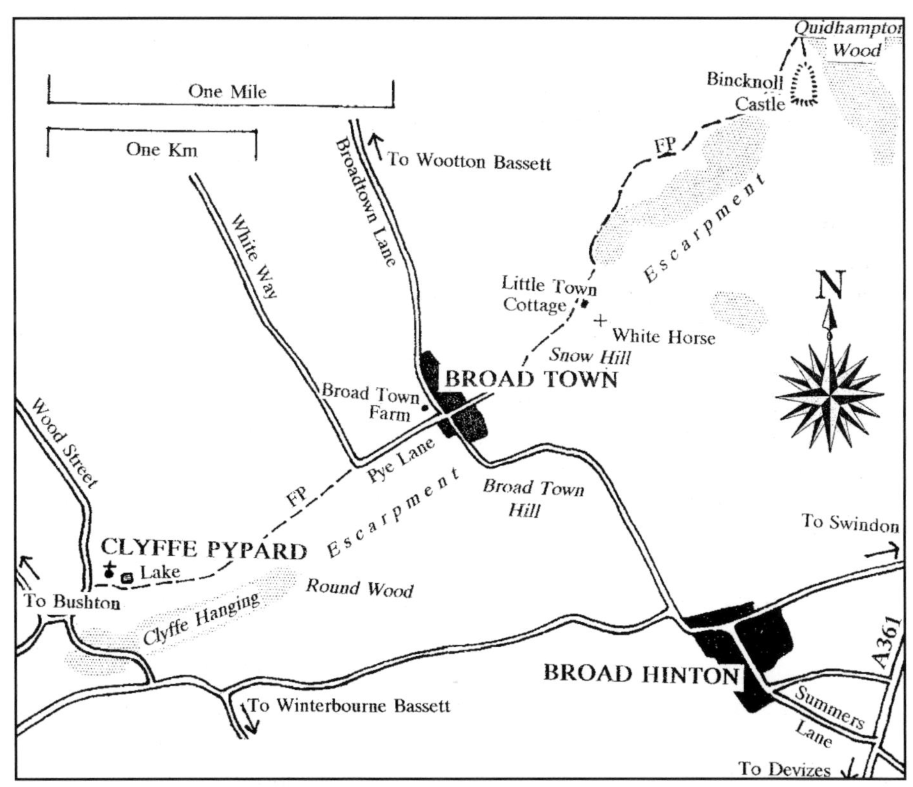

Escarpment: Clyffe Pypard to Bincknoll

Above: Little Town with left to right Little Town Farm, White Horse, and Pevsner's cottage;

Below: Little Town Farmhouse from the escarpment, showing the view from near Pevsner's cottage.

Bincknoll Castle

From Little Town the path continues first north and then north-east over ground much disturbed by chalk diggings between the wooded escarpment to the right and the wide views over the plain to the left to Bincknoll Castle (107793). This 'castle' had been an Iron Age promontory hillfort which was adapted as a Norman castle which has now entirely vanished. It was described by Pevsner as a 'Motte and bailey castle on a chalk promontory, the top having been scarped off to form the motte'. Hippisley Cox in *The Green Roads of England* (1914) referred to 'the destroyed camp of Bincknol' and suggested that it was related to Barbury Castle a little over three miles to its south-east. He also noted that it had 'suffered much from the falling away of the cliff'. It is no coincidence that the farm to the south-east of Bincknoll is called Sandfurlong Farm for the ground in this area is sandy and unstable and has a history of landslips occurring on its steep slopes. Such a landslip which destroyed part of an ancient manor house was described in Volume 1 of *Wiltshire Notes and Queries*. The instability of the ground in this area may have contributed to the disappearance without trace of the Norman Castle.

Alternatively, the disappearance of Bincknoll Castle may be explained on historical grounds. Norman castles were private fortresses built and held by landowners, who had become vassals of the king in return for extensive grants of land. The early castles were therefore effectively controlled by the king, but as time went by they sometimes became bases for revolt against the royal authority. They were designed to be a base from which a small number of mounted armoured men could dominate a considerable area. It was not unusual for a Norman castle to avail itself of an existing prehistoric earthwork, as was the case here at Bincknoll where the Iron Age fort became the 'bailey' (the outer enclosure). A 'motte', which was a mound surmounted by a tower or keep of timber or stone was then superimposed on the ancient earthwork. The early timber keeps tended to be replaced by stone because of their vulnerability to fire, both accidental and when assaulted. After the chaotic disturbances of the reign (1135-54) of Stephen, when the *Anglo-Saxon Chronicle* recorded that castles wer 'filled with devils and evil men' who indulged in extorting money by unspeakable tortures', the new king Henry II attempted to pacify England by destroying many castles which were potential bases for revolt, and it may have been early in his reign (1154-1189) that Bincknoll Castle was destroyed. Such a short life could explain the absence of records of this castle.

Bincknoll Castle is best approached from the north by the earthen ramp which was probably formed as the approach to the original castle gate. The

Above: Bincknoll Castle from Bincknoll Dip;

Below: Bincknoll Dip looking north-west with Bincknoll Castle (left) and Quidhampton Wood (right)

castle seems to have no recorded history and may have been built by the powerful Bishop Odo of Bayeux who owned both Woodhill four miles south-west of Bincknoll and Swindon five miles to its north-east. The Bishop, as half brother to the Conqueror, was a major landowner in this area and may have constructed an early castle at Bincknoll – perhaps of timber availing itself of a ready-made prehistoric site – to overawe the recently conquered Saxons. Bincknoll may then have declined early or changed hands when Odo was exiled by Rufus in the late 11th century.

It is relevant to note that in 1332 Bincknoll paid more in tax than either Highway, Broad Town or Clyffe Pypard, most of it being paid by Lord John de Cobham. Bincknoll or its site may later have come into the hands of the Lovel family who owned Elcombe deer park (133810) two miles north-east of Bincknoll. As early as 1242 Ralph Lovel held a knight's fee at Clyffe Pypard of Walter de Dunstanville, and he or his descendants may have held land at Bincknoll which is situated between the Lovel lands at Clyffe Pypard and Elcombe. John Lovel certainly owned Elcombe Park in the 13th century and his descendant John, the 2nd Lord Lovel, was in 1272 governor of Marlborough Castle. The Lovel estates were forfeited when Francis 11th Lord Lovel remained loyal to Richard III when Henry Tudor usurped his throne and established the Tudor dynasty on the throne of England in 1485 (further information on the Lovels will be provided in Chapter 8 of volume 2 under Upton Lovell).

Before leaving Bincknoll it is well worth looking into the deep cleft called Bincknoll Dip (108793) beneath the steep ramparts of Bincknoll Castle which forms an elongated natural amphitheatre which I imagine may have been a jousting ground for the castle. Here, looking down into Bincknoll Dip from the heights of the castle, I recall watching a buzzard in flight from above. From Bincknoll Castle there are also splendid views to the three clumps of beeches which stand beside the Ridgeway on Hackpen Hill three miles away to the south-west and provide distinctive landmarks from so many parts of north-east Wiltshire.

The main downland escarpment ends at the great promontory of Bincknoll Castle where the great cleft of Bincknoll Dip, which contains the source of a stream that runs north-west, cuts into the downs and separates Bincknoll Castle from Quidhampton Wood to its east. The sight of the towering bluffs of Bincknoll Castle seen from the floor of Bincknoll Dip at the west end of Quidhampton Wood is a dramatic experience that should not be missed.

Although the escarpment continues north-east beyond Bincknoll Dip its continuation is on a reduced scale and is less evident, being obscured by the hanging woods of Quidhampton Wood. Within this wood it adopts a slight turn to run east and gradually reduces and fades away. After the escarpment leaves Salthrop Wood and crosses the little road from Elcombe to the A4361 on Wroughton Hill – described by Edward Thomas as 'one of the most lovable of the roads from the hills to the elm country' – it becomes insignificant by comparison with its scale between Highway and Bincknoll, and it effectively expires as it approaches Wroughton Church perched high on its eminence at the extreme south-west edge of its village. This comment is not intended to disparage this area towards Wroughton which consists of fine countryside that is well worth walking, with Clouts Wood – now a nature reserve – on the opposite side of the A4361 in a deep coombe under the former Wroughton aerodrome.

The area which I have designated Grigson Country and described in this chapter has many virtues including a distinctive remoteness which makes it an excellent place to walk for those who seek secluded walks in an attractive and quite unspoilt but practically unknown area of Wiltshire.

Clyffe Pypard church from south-west.

Suggested Walks in Grigson Country

4A: Clyffe Pypard to Bincknoll (7 miles: map 173):

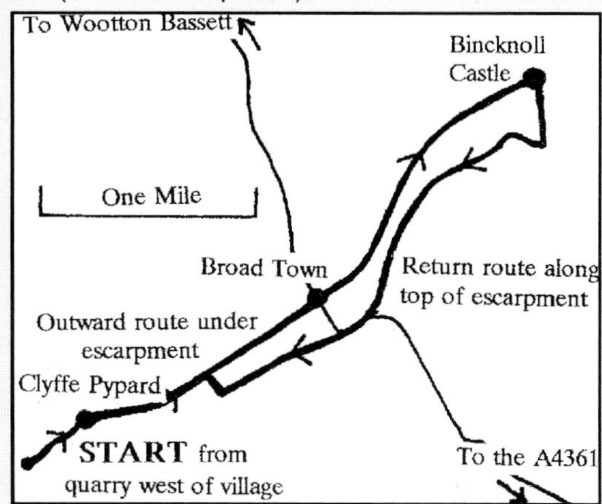

Without doubt the most interesting walking in Grigson Country is along the foot of the escarpment from Clyffe Pypard to Bincknoll which has a character quite distinct from any other in Wiltshire. A fine walk of about six miles may be taken by parking at Clyffe Pypard (parking in the village is difficult but is possible a little south-west of the village near the site of a former quarry at about 071766) and walking east through the churchyard past Pevsner's grave and the lake and along the the foot of the escarpment from Clyffe Pypard as far as Bincknoll Castle. After climbing the escarpment by the footpath which runs south up the ramp (107794) to the site of the castle the return may be over the outgoing route under the escarpment or along the footpaths which follow the top of the escarpment along the upper edge of Bincknoll Wood and above Little Town and offer intermittent long views over the broad lowland plain towards Malmesbury. The descent of the escarpment to return to the line of the outgoing scarp foot route may be effected at either Little Town White Horse, at Broad Town Hill a mile and a half from Clyffe Pypard, or at the north-east end of Clyffe Hanging half a mile from Clyffe Pypard.

4B: Wroughton to Binknoll (5 miles: map 173):

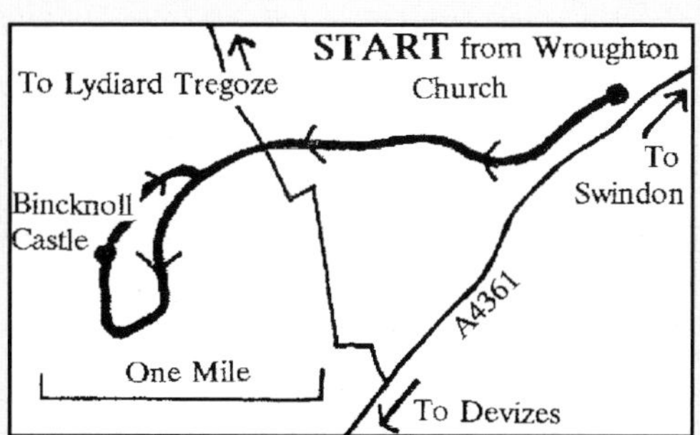

Quidhampton Wood to the north-east of Bincknoll Castle has footpaths along both its lower (north-west) and its upper (south-east) edges, the latter running a few yards within the wood rather than along its very edge as shown on the map. These footpaths may be incorporated, one as the outer and the other as the return path, into an extension of the above walk from Clyffe Pypard to Bincknoll. They may also be incorporated in a five mile mixed downland and woodland walk from the car park beside Wroughton Church to Bincknoll Castle.

4C: Clyffe Pypard to Highway (5 miles: map 173):
Similar walks, although not so interesting as the walks just described, may be followed along the south-west end of the escarpment from Clyffe Pypard towards Highway past Bupton and Clevancy

4D: Bincknoll to the Ridgeway (9 miles; map 173):
Towards the north end of the escarp-ment from near Bincknoll Castle it is feasible to walk from Bincknoll to the Ridgeway on Hackpen Hill, following the public footpaths which cross the three miles (as the crow flies) of country-side between the outer and inner escarp-ments of the Marl-borough Downs. Bincknoll Castle is accessible by a road running south-east from the A420 east of Wootton Bassett. The route of the walk is south from Bincknoll Castle through The Weir (113771 on the A361), half a mile north-east along the minor road towards Uffcott, turning at 122772 south-east and reaching Hackpen by the straight footpath which is aligned on the most northern of the three Hackpen beech clumps. The climb up Hackpen Hill is very sharp. The opportunities for varying the return route are rather restricted, but the return back to Bincknoll may be by another footpath which runs from 144764 west of Barbury Castle north-west over Uffcott Down between the hangars of Wroughton airfield and Uffcott village.

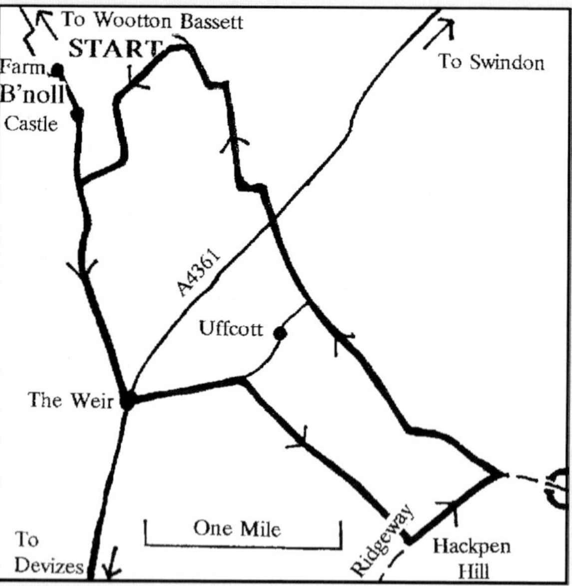

The minor road which crosses the A4361 and passes Salthrop Farm is then followed as far as Quidhampton Wood, where the footpath along the south and south-east edge of the wood is taken back to Bincknoll.

4E: Highway to the Ridgeway

(7.5 or 9 miles if the walker is met as indicated):

Walks from the Highway area to the Ridgeway may follow any of the several alternative footpaths which run along the former droveways south-east from Highway and Clevancy over the flat plain between the upper and lower escarpments of the Marlborough Downs across 'The Vize Way', now known as Yatesbury Lane (067734) but surviving as a public right of way. At this southern end of the district described in this chapter the two escarpments have diverged farther apart and walking the entire distance between them and back is more arduous, unless the walker can arrange to be picked up at the end of the walk. In this case Yatesbury Lane can be crossed and the walk continued through Winterbourne Monkton, crossing the A4361 and following Mill Lane eastwards past the former windmill site at Windmill House and the quarry at its end (107726) and over Winterbourne Down with its complex of prehistoric field monuments to the Ridgeway near Glory Ann (127727). From Highway to Glory Ann is 6 miles. The walker may then be met by a car at either the road crossing of Hackpen Hill a mile and a half to the north of Glory Ann, or at the A4 on Overton Hill, which is reached by walking 3 miles south from Glory Ann down the Ridgeway (described in Chapter 1).

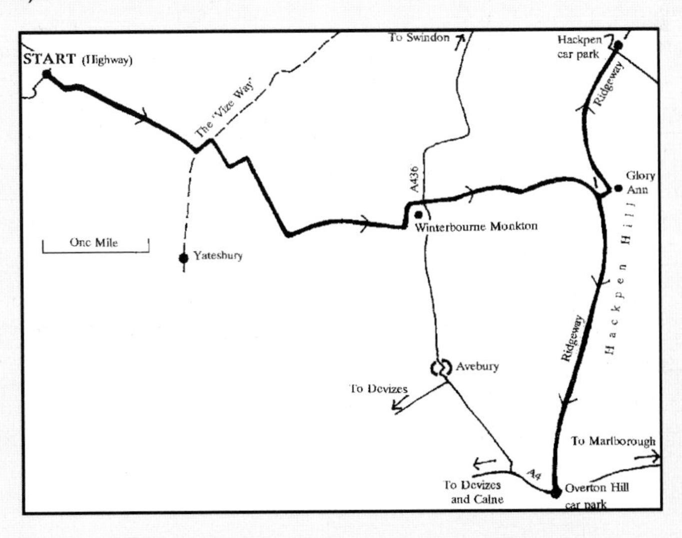

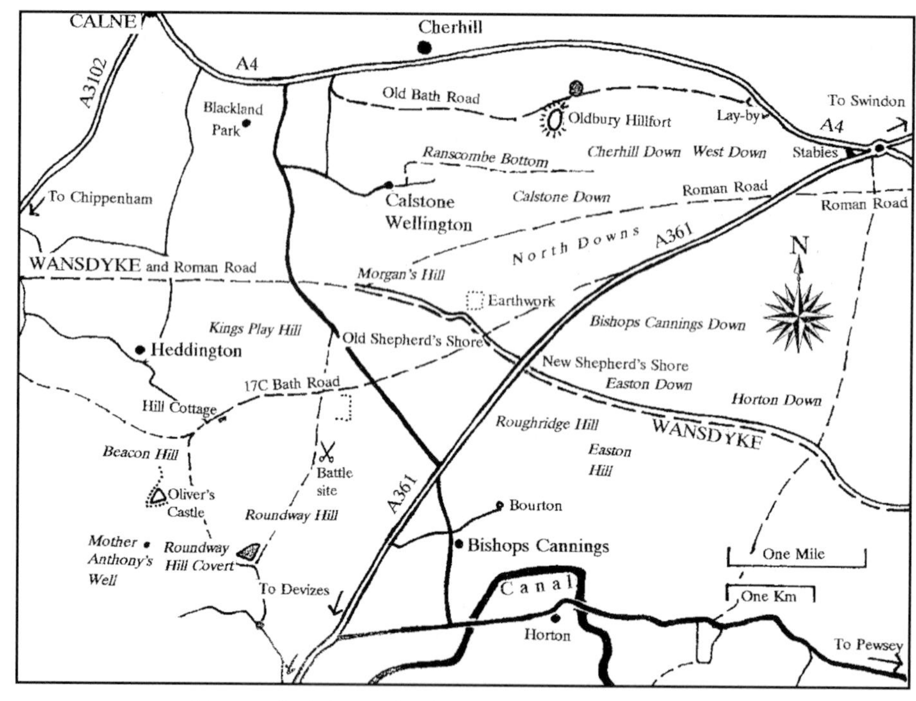

Above: Calstone, Oldbury and Roundway Down;

Below: Natural erosion gullies between Beacon Hill and Oliver's Castle

5 Calstone, Oldbury and Roundway Down:
The South-West Marlborough Downs

(map Landranger 173)

This chapter describes the arm of the Marlborough Downs which extends south-west from the main block of the downs from Avebury towards Devizes and is contained within the triangle formed by the A4 Beckhampton-Calne road, the A361 between Beckhampton and Devizes, and its western escarpment at Oliver's Castle and Roundway Covert Hill. It is an area rich in history and prehistory, containing a Roman road, several successive lines of the former coach road from London to Bath, a section of the massive ancient frontier of Wansdyke, many prehistoric monuments including the Iron Age fortresses of Oldbury and Oliver's Castles, the site of the Civil War battle of Roundway Down, and the secluded village of Calstone Wellington. This village provides a good base from which to walk the area, for example east up the little-frequented coombes which offer delightful walking eastwards to Oldbury Castle and the obelisk known as the Lansdowne (or Cherhill) Monument. Other convenient points from which to commence walks over this area are the Smallgrain Plantation picnic site (019672) near the golf course , and the large lay-by beside the A4 a little west of Beckhampton roundabout.

The Western Escarpment

The dramatic escarpment formed at the west end of this area by Beacon Hill, Oliver's Castle, and the west end of Roundway Hill at Roundway Hill Covert is effectively the extreme south-western escarpment of this outlying area of the Marlborough Downs. Between Oliver's Castle and Beacon Hill the great bare indent in the hillside has in the distant past been naturally sculpted by melt waters flowing off the Roundway plateau into the fantastic moulded shapes which are such a distinctive feature of this landscape. This lumpy sculpted landscape resembles the uneven background to Paul Nash's fine painting 'Wood on the Downs' (1930) – which actually is based on Ivinghoe Beacon in Buckinghamshire – although except for Roundway Hill Covert south of Oliver's Castle the escarpment generally lacks in trees. There are however a few wind-harassed bare-stemmed beeches on Oliver's Castle hillfort, and a narrow scrubby copse of trees, including yew and juniper, accompany the former turnpiked road down the western slope of Beacon Hill. Apart from these the downland escarpment is bare of trees except for the scatters of the 'wind-warped upland thorns' on its precipitous hillsides.

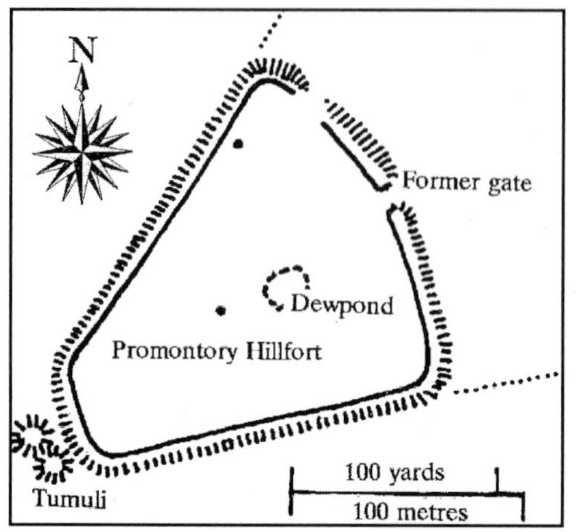

Another noticeable feature of this escarpment is the sere buff colour which it invariably assumes in winter. In my experience sheep never graze the steep slopes of Oliver's Castle or Beacon Hill and it is likely that the distinctive light dun winter colour of these downs arises from the absence of sheep, a consequence of this being that the grass is never cropped into the short green downland turf that William Stukeley admired and described as being 'like a Turkey carpet'. Here the grass is allowed to grow rank and long and the withered tufts and bents mask the green grass below, giving these hillsides their distinctive dead colour in winter.

Although this dramatically modelled landscape may be seen from above from the north edge of Oliver's Castle, it is at its most dramatic when viewed from below from the footpath which runs north from Consciences Lane (west of Roundway village) to Beacon Hill, and more distantly from near Trowbridge in west Wiltshire. From these directions the immense series of drainage furrows down the hillside make a marked contrast with the horizontal strip lynchets that follow the escarpment around Oliver's Castle at a low level. This escarpment, which is quite unsurpassed in Wiltshire, is at its most dramatic when seen on a late sunny summer evening or in low winter sunshine when the slanting light emphasises the incredible forms of the landscape.

At the foot of the hill below Oliver's Castle the melt waters have gouged a huge ditch about twenty feet deep that is almost a small ravine and is known as Bloody Ditch from its Civil War associations, when it impeded the flight of the Parliamentary cavalry and sharp fighting took place around it.

Calstone Wellington Village

This secluded and little-known village is situated two miles south-east of Calne at the head of the tiny River Marden. A little east of Calstone a lake has formed in a steep gorge at the head of the river, which flows north-east through Blacklands and Calne to join the River Avon near Chippenham. The delightful name of Calstone Wellington – twin element names always seem to be attractive – probably derives its first element from Calne and its second from the family of Ralphe de Wilinton who was an early owner of the manor. In Domesday it was *Calstone*, and today the village is generally known by that single-element name.

Calstone is so secluded that it has been missed or ignored by nearly all the topographical writers on Wiltshire, and yet it was formerly a place of considerable activity with no less than four mills driven by the little Marden stream. One was a flour mill, and another a paper mill driven by a large water wheel which stood at an outlet from the pool. There was also a snuff mill, and at the west end of the village the three-storeyed building known as Sprays which was demolished after the Second World War was at one time Sprays Mill, run by the Edwards family as a woollen mill. Later it went over to manufacturing mop heads. Calstone Mill, to the north of the village, is a fine building with a Grade Two listed 19th century malthouse. Of the four farms which formerly existed at Calstone – Sprays Farm, Manor Farm, East Farm and South Farm – only Manor Farm survives as a working farm.

A local cottage industry was the production of whitening. A dewpond maker called Edwin Green lived in a cottage at Calstone and ran a whitening ring using a pony to haul a millstone round and round in a large round stone trough to crush chalk which was then rolled by hand by the women of the village into small spheres and sold for whitening cottage walls, hearthstones, and thresholds. Upstream from the lake withies for basket-making were grown, and there were watercress beds.

Calstone Pool was also used as a sheep-washing pool and the gorge was consequently known as Washpool Bottom, although Andrews and Dury in 1773 marked the river towards the head of the gorge 'Godwins Head'. The washpool was leased by Isaac Smith and Mark Ponting who would stand in tarred barrels to keep dry when washing the thousands of sheep from all over the district which would descend on Calstone to be washed in late May or early June, for nowhere else in the area was to be found such an ample and constant supply of running water, the sound of which permeates the gorge above Calstone.

Calstone was a home of the Ducketts, a family which owned the manor of Calne and other extensive estates in this area. They had a manor house on the site of the present Manor Farm which was destroyed in the Civil War, presumably in July 1643 when the battle was fought on nearby Roundway Down.

The small church of St Mary at Calstone stands down a side lane at the southern extremity of the village with adjoining 'humps and bumps' in the field to its west. Although Andrews and Dury show the church as already isolated on their 1773 map of Wiltshire, these earthworks suggest that at one time part of the village may have been located around its church and later moved away. On the exterior of the north wall of the church is an early-19th century memorial tablet to a former stagecoach driver on the London to Bath road which ran across Cherhill Down. His amusing inscription reads

While passengers of every age
With care I drove from stage to stage,
Death's sable hearse pass'd by unseen,
And stop'd the course of my machine.

Roman Road

Half-a-mile south of Calstone church the Roman road from Marlborough to Bath ran across the downs after passing Silbury Hill and crossing the present A361 near Beckhampton Buildings (at 075684) where it is still visible to the east of the A361 as a grassy *agger* aligned on Silbury Hill. Despite having been ploughed, this Roman road over North Down is readily discernible with a series of quarry pits which provided material for the road.

Roman road on Calstone Down looking west.

To the north of Morgan's Hill several ways run north from this road to the gorge at the east end of Calstone. The Roman road remains a public right of way, as do some of these paths to Calstone. It seems likely that the Romans, from this point four miles from their wells at Swallowhead Springs near Silbury, and another four miles from their station at *Verlucio* (Sandy Lane), may have sometimes diverted from their road to rest and refresh themselves and their animals at the Calstone springs. A mile further west the Roman road, after running along a terrace past Horsecombe Bottom (027673), is joined by Wansdyke. In 1808 William Cunnington excavated a section east of Smallgrain Plantation (at 023672) where the Roman road and Wansdyke coincide and established that the Roman road was older than Wansdyke. Eighty years later, in 1889, General Pitt Rivers also sectioned Wansdyke a little east of Furze Knoll (at 035668).

Wansdyke and Old Shepherd's Shore

The vastly impressive post-Roman bank and ditch frontier called Wansdyke, one of the greatest linear earthworks in Britain, crosses this area from Morgan's Hill to the A361. (The stretch of Wansdyke immediately to the east of this area has been described in Chapter 3). South-east of Morgan's Hill the point where Wansdyke is breached by the former London to Bath road is known as Old Shepherd's Shore (040666), 'shore' being an old word for a gap. At one time an inn called the Shepherd's Rest stood nearby. The 'Shepherds' Bench Lawns' of the 17th century Court Books probably commemorated a seat on which the shepherds gossiped and enjoyed their ale, and the 'Gallows Breach Lands' of the Tithe Award suggests that a gallows also existed near Old Shepherd's Shore.

The large rectangular earthwork (040671) situated a little north of Old Shepherd's Shore measuring about 240 yards (220m) square has been proved by excavation to be medieval in date and was probably a permanent penning which provided protection for sheep and their shepherds in extreme weather on these exposed downs.

One June day in 1613 George Ferebe, the rector of Bishops Cannings who had aspirations to being a poet, arranged for his parishioners to entertain Queen Anne at Old Shepherd's Shore on her return from taking the waters at Bath. Ferebe wrote a song for his parishioners to sing in which there was a reference to the 'wild, wide, houseless downs' of this area. A taste of the quality of the entertainment is contained in the lines :

Stand still, great queen, amidst your loving people,
And listen to the bells of Bishops Cannings steeple.

George Ferebe had the text of his entertainment printed and sent copies to London where they were circulated at Court. John Aubrey records that the queen received her rustic entertainment very graciously, and its text is preserved in the Aubrey manuscripts at the Bodleian Library in Oxford.

Five years after Queen Anne's visit James I (in 1618) passed along the old road through Old Shepherd's Shore during one of his many visits to Wiltshire, on this occasion on his way to Bromham to Sir Edward Bayntun's Bromham House for the hunting.

The point where the present main road – the A361 – breaches Wansdyke is New Shepherd's Shore. Here was a former inn which was believed to be the scene of 'The Bagman's Story' in the *Pickwick Papers* (1837) by Charles Dickens (1812-70). The building, which stood on the north side of the road and was shown on the first edition of the Ordnance Survey, declined to a cottage and was demolished as recently as the early 1990s.

The Old Bath Road: Shepherd's Shore to Beacon Hill

After leaving Old Shepherd's Shore the early line of the Bath Road ran westwards where its 18th century milestones can still be found in the hedges on the south side of the way. Immediately west of Old Shepherd's Shore a branch from the Bath Road ran south-west to Devizes, passing near Hill Barn Cottages (033654) and over Stone Pit Hill where another inn or beer house existed among the trees on the existing hedged lane. The first half mile (from 037664) of this Devizes branch is now a hedgeline and is no longer a right of way, although the lane over Stone Pit Hill remains a designated bridleway.

The original Bath Mail Coach, 1784.

The main line of the road passed Hill Cottage (formerly Hill Farm at 069657) and descended Beacon Hill, a hill so steep that for the eastwards journey to London extra horses were kept nearby to help in dragging the coaches up the hill. In its descent of Beacon Hill the turnpike passed a little north of the site of the former Bayntun mansion of Bromham House, now Bromham House Farm. Bromham House was built in the 16th century by the Bayntuns who acquired Bromham by marriage into the Roche family, having previously been at Faulston, part of Bishopstone in south Wiltshire.

North-east side of Beacon Hill above Heddington from King's Play Hill

The Bayntuns became established at Court. Sir Edward Bayntun (d.1545) was vice-chamberlain to four of Henry VIII's queens – a not inconsiderable achievement as they successively came into and went out of favour. He was entrusted with obtaining confessions from men accused of having had treasonable relations with Queen Ane Boleyn, and was both brother-in-law and governor of the household to Catherine Howard who was Henry VIII's queen from 1540 to 1543.

Bromham House was financed by the combined spoils of the Dissolution of the monasteries, the old house at Corsham, and materials from Devizes Castle. The house was a splendid one, described by Leland as 'nearly as large as Whitehall and fit to entertain a king'. This function it performed on a number of occasions. In 1535 Sir Edward Bayntun entertained Henry VIII and his court at Bromham, and early in the 17th century the town records of Devizes record several visits by James I to Bromham, in 1613, 1618, and 1623. These royal visits were almost certainly to take advantage of the hunting in the park for we know that James I was a passionate hunter and that when staying at Bromham he once slew a buck near Lackham Park, then owned by Sir Robert Bayard. Bromham House, which is passed by a public footpath which runs from Turnpike Farm on the old coach road to the A342 near Bromham village was, like Calstone Manor, destroyed in the Civil War.

At the bottom of Beacon Hill, near Sandy Lane the Bath Road passed Bear Farm and Bell Farm (972672), both once inns on the road, The Bear being for the travellers and The Bell a humbler establishment for their servants and the coachmen.

This early line of the Bath Road through Shepherd's Shore and Sandy Lane was finally abandoned in about 1755 for a new route that will be described later (page 132-4).

Battle of Roundway Down

Early in the English Civil War an event of national importance took place near Old Shepherd's Shore when the Battle of Roundway Down was fought on 13 July 1643. During the 'royalist summer' of 1643 the Royalists were experiencing great success and King Charles ordered his armies to concentrate at his headquarters at Oxford for an assault on London. After leading the Royalist Western Army out of the west Lord Hopton, having fought an inconclusive action with a Parliamentary army under Sir William Waller at Lansdown Hill near Bath on 5 July, found himself besieged by Waller in Devizes, afraid to continue eastwards over the open downs because of his inferiority in cavalry. At midnight on 10-11 July the Royalist cavalry succeeded in breaking out of Devizes and riding to Oxford to summon help. On 11 July King Charles dispatched a relief column consisting of about eighteen hundred cavalry and two small field guns under Prince Maurice and Lord Wilmot.

This column approached Devizes from Marlborough on 13 July through Beckhampton along the road which crossed Wansdyke at Old Shepherd's Shore. Hearing of their approach Waller withdrew his army, consisting of 1800-2500 infantry, 2000 cavalry, 500 dragoons (mounted infantry) and from seven to nine cannon, from investing Devizes and formed them into battle order a little west of the Bishops Cannings to Calne road between King's Play Down and the east end of Roundway Down, then known as Bagnall

Hill. The ensuing battle took place in the area enclosed by King's Play Down, Morgan's Hill, Roughridge Hill, and Oliver's Castle – a misnomer as Oliver Cromwell was at this time neither a leading figure, nor was he present at Roundway Down.

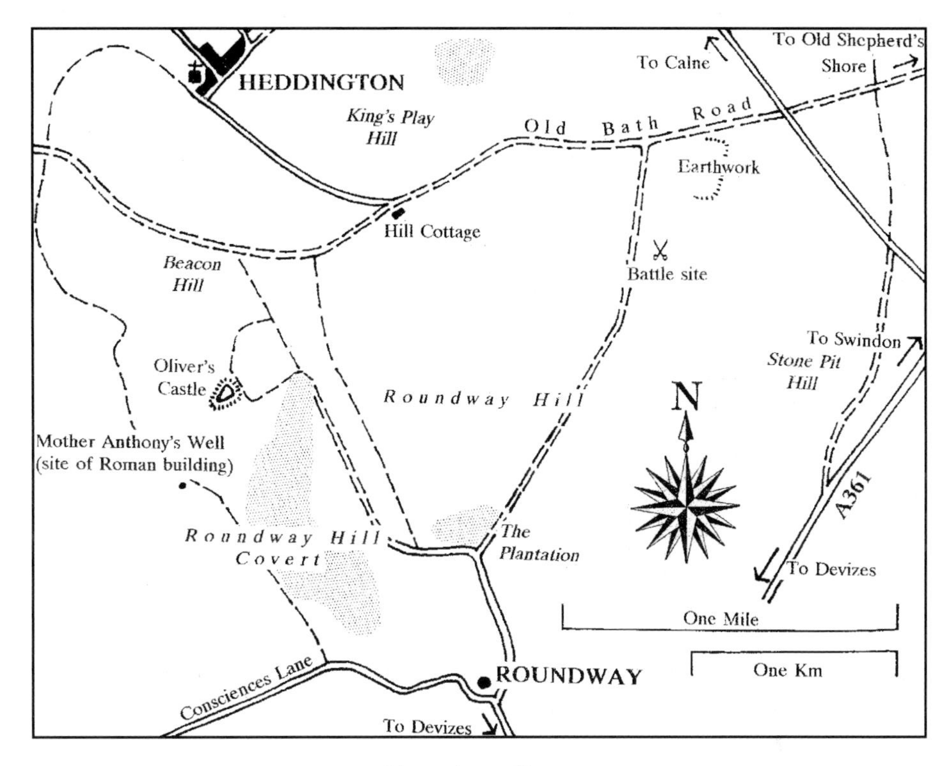

Roundway Down

After crossing Wansdyke and approaching within sight of the Parliamentary army formed up on the eastern slopes of Roundway Hill to their west, the Royalist cavalry formed up into battle order to the west of the dyke, straddling both the coach road at Old Shepherd's Shore and the present A361 which did not then exist. They engaged and soon dispersed the entire Parliamentary cavalry after Lord Wilmot's brigade put to flight Sir Arthur Haselrig's heavy armoured cavalry known as the 'Lobsters'. Armour at this time was going out of fashion – hence the mocking 'Lobster' nickname. After the Parliamentary cavalry had been dispersed their commander was pursued across the downs by Richard Atkyns who later wrote the history of Gloucestershire. Atkyns left an account of how he repeatedly chopped at Haselrig with his sword and fired a pistol into his side, all to no effect because of his heavy armour. When later told of this incident King Charles commented wryly: 'Had he been provisioned he could have withstood a siege'. The defeated Parliamentary horse fled westwards down the steep slopes around Oliver's Castle and Roundway Hill Covert. The deep ditch below Oliver's Castle known as Bloody Ditch (998649) has yielded military equipmemt from this period. The immense scale of the escarpment which towers over Bloody Ditch dwarfs the ditch when seen from above. If visited it will be found to be a considerable ditch about 20 feet (6 m) in depth. The abandoned Parliamentary infantry resisted for a time but, demoralised by the flight of their cavalry, threw down their arms when Hopton's Royalist infantry began to march out of Devizes and arrive on the downs through Roundway village.

Looking down gully over Bloody Ditch (centre)

This battle was decisive in that it led to the fall of the important city and port of Bristol to the Royalists a few days later. It was unusual in that a column of light cavalry succeeded in emphatically defeating a balanced army more than twice its size consisting of infantry, cavalry and artillery. The key to the action is that the Royalist cavalry succeeded in defeating Waller's superior army in detail by dispersing his cavalry before he could bring his infantry and guns into effective action. After the battle was over Lord Wilmot and Prince Maurice compared their commissions and discovered that Lord Wilmot was the senior officer, and he was consequently given the credit for the victory.

Roman Villa and Mother Anthony's Well

At the western extremity of this area, near the point where the Parliamentary cavalry were pursued over the escarpment, stands Oliver's Castle, a small Iron Age promontory fort enclosing merely three acres. Below it was a Roman building, probably a villa, on the site of a spring now known as Mother Anthony's Well (999643). During many years of researching Wiltshire local history I have have never seen this strange place-name mentioned or explained. It is interesting to speculate whether this spring was the source of water for the Roman building, and if that building had a shrine dedicated to St Anthony (251-356 AD), a saint of the Romano-British period who founded the first Christian monastery, at Memphis, the old capital of Egypt and lived to be a hundred and five. Here beside Mother Anthony's Well substantial foundation walls are known to exist, Roman pottery and other objects have been found, and many *tesserae* from broken up mosaic pavements have appeared on the site which is outlined by crop marks in dry weathers, as on the occasion recorded by Canon Goddard in 1907.

An alternative explanation for the name of Mother Anthony's Well may lie in the fact that in the insanitary Middle Ages skin diseases were common. Such a disease (erysipelas) was then known as St Antony's Fire. Near Micheldean in Gloucestershire a St Antony's Well was used for bathing to cure St Antony's Fire which it was believed could be cured by the intercession of St Antony. Could the name Mother Anthony's Well under Oliver's Castle be a corruption of a St Antony's Well to which skin disease sufferers resorted for a cure in the Middle Ages?

The existence of this Roman building near Mother Anthony's Well is probably explained by Roman activity around Bromham to exploit the iron ore of this district. There is other evidence of the Roman presence under the Oliver's Castle escarpment. A Roman villa was found beside the A342 in Bromham Park (973658) and the name Netherstreet (982655) is suggestive as the place-name 'street' in a country district generally indicates the existence of a Roman road, and Netherstreet is merely two miles south-east of the Roman station of *Verlucio* at Sandy Lane. This site is accessible by a public footpath which runs along the foot of the escarpment from Consciences Lane (006634) near Roundway village to Heddington, and passes near Bloody Ditch which is mentioned above in the account of the Battle of Roundway Down on page 126.

South of Oliver's Castle part of the steep escarpment overlooking Mother Anthony's Well is occupied by Roundway Hill Covert, a wood which is now accessible since it has been designated a nature reserve.

Barrow with standing stone on West Down with Silbury Hill in background

Prehistoric Barrows and Strip-Lynchets

Two Neolithic long barrows exist in these south-west Marlborough Downs, one on the crest of King's Play Hill, the other south of Old Shepherd's Shore (at 038661). Many Bronze Age tumuli are scattered over these downs although coincidentally many of them are aside from the public rights of way and are therefore inaccessible and only visible at a distance. On North Down are two rows of four tumuli (at 043677 and 046678) and a cluster known as Three Barrows which are accessible being beside the point (058674) where the old road diverges from the A361. Other round barrows are scattered in pairs or stand in isolation all over the area, some of them being prominently situated on the skyline of North Down when seen from the A361. One round barrow in a beech copse beside the Roman road on West Down (at 070683) has the unusual feature of a four feet high slender sarsen stone standing at its centre which is just visible from the A361. This stone appears to be a redundant gatepost erected by a landowner in recent times. King's Play Hill has strip lynchets on its eastern slopes, and other vestiges of strip-lynchets occur on the western slopes of Oliver's Castle. The downs are also scored by a variety of unexplained prehistoric linear earthworks.

Calstone village is a delightful place to visit in spring when the small birds are active in the woods which clothe the steep sides of the gorge, and water oozes and gushes from the springs in the rock face on its north side. The lane known as Lovers' Walk, which runs behind the cottage on the north side of the gorge at Calstone, runs on westwards, becomes a footpath, and then enters Ranscombe Bottom. This long shallow coombe is associated with a delightful series of other secluded and interlinked cross coombes that run up to the Lansdowne Monument, the ponderous and not very elegant obelisk that dominates the landscape of this area. The monument was erected in the 1840s to commemorates Sir William Petty (1623-87), an ancestor of the Lansdowne family who was a man of many talents. In his youth William Petty went to sea and was abandoned in France where he set up as a merchant and educated himself. He then returned to England and became both Professor of Anatomy at Brasenose College and Professor of Music at Gresham College at Oxford. He achieved great celebrity by reviving Nan Green, a woman who had been hanged for murdering her child. His many talents made Petty one of John Aubrey's 'chiefest freinds'. He was the subject of one of Aubrey's *Brief Lives*, and was described by Aubrey as 'that ingeniose and great Virtuoso, Sir William Petty'. Having become also a celebrated political economist, Petty was appointed by the Commonwealth Parliament to survey Ireland, and as a result of these activities acquired vast estates in Ireland which founded the fortunes of the Lansdowne family. Aubrey testified to the 'sweet disposition' of his talented friend, and tells us that before he went to Ireland he practiced as a solicitor. At the Restoration in 1660 Sir William returned to England and, despite having worked for Parliament during the Commonwealth, became a favourite with Charles II who enjoyed his conversation. In England he invented a double-hulled ship designed to be unsinkable, but it was lost in a storm in the Irish Sea! He wrote influential works on political economy, and was described by the diarist John Evelyn as the best living Latin poet. Sir William Petty died of a gangrenous foot at the age of 64 and is buried in Romsey Abbey.

An amusing tale was recorded by Aubrey about Sir William Petty, who was particularly short-sighted. After being challenged to a duel by a celebrated soldier Petty, having the right as the challenged to nominate the venue and the weapons, chose a darkened cellar and carpenter's axes, ridiculing his opponent into withdrawing his challenge.

The Lansdowne Monument was designed by Sir Charles Barry (1795-1860) who designed extensive alterations at Bowood for the third Earl of Lansdowne and later designed the Houses of Parliament.

In 1991 the monument was rescued from a derelict condition and rebuilt by The National Trust which owns much of the land around Oldbury Castle.

Cherhill White Horse and Lansdowne Monument from Cherhill.

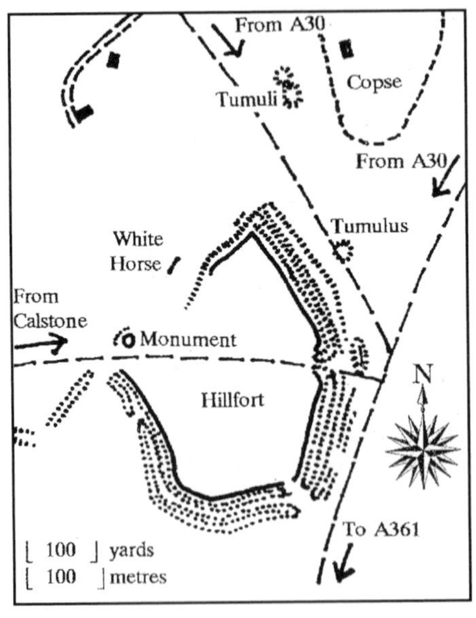

Oldbury Castle Hillfort

This hillfort is roughly triangular and encloses about twenty acres. It has been extensively damaged by flint digging and by the excavation of chalk to refurbish the Cherhill White Horse which was constructed in 1780 on the west face of Cherhill Down beneath Oldbury Castle facing west towards Calne. Since most of the land around Oldbury belongs to The National Trust it is freely accessible. From the hillfort the views are oustanding, south over the coombes, and north-west over Avebury into the Marlborough Downs with the distant Hackpen beech clumps prominent beside the Ridgeway on Hackpen Hill.

Calstone Coombes

The land in the series of interlinking coombes east of Calstone was intensively worked on the medieval system of growing arable crops on both the strip-lynchets on the hillsides and in fields running up the coombe sides until well into the eighteenth century. The strips, together with the names of their holders, are recorded on a Bowood estate map. Today the lynchets may still be seen running along the interlinking coombe sides. The hillsides are also scored by the horizontal lines of terracettes which are the natural result of slippage of the thin topsoil down the slopes of the hillsides. These terracettes are often followed by sheep which are consequently sometimes mistakenly believed to have worn them. The downs around Ranscombe Bottom contain some patches of juniper scrub, which is now becoming rare. One embanked enclosure on the north flank of Ranscombe Bottom (at 043685) is probably the remains of a medium sized 18th century tree ring which may once have enclosed a copse.

Calstone Coombes from near Oldbury Castle

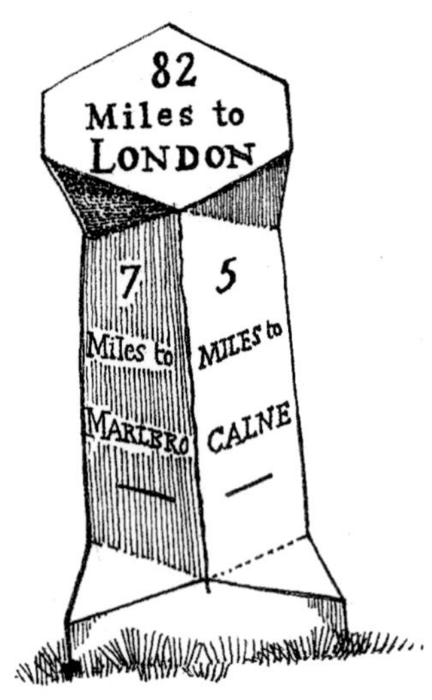

The Old Bath Road over Cherhill Down

The later history of this area is very much bound up with that of the Old Bath Road which crossed the district from Beckhampton, along which all of English society would have travelled from the time in about 1700 when Bath became popular as a spa to the coming of the railway in 1840. The Old Bath Coach Road crossed these downs along various routes. In its early days in the 17th century it ran as described earlier through Old Shepherd's Shore, but by the early 18th century it had been re-routed north of the Roman road along the southern slopes of Cherhill Down probably to avoid the steep descent of Beacon Hill. In rough weather this route was very exposed to the prevailing wind and the *Bath Journal* recorded many accidents attributable to the wind such as coaches being overturned and coachmen being blown from their boxes. Earthen banks ten feet high constructed to provide shelter may still be seen, covered with stunted shrubs.

An illustration of the power of storms in this area was demonstrated when a storm of exceptional violence crossed this district on 29 December 1859. The storm started in Bowood Park and reached its climax at Blacklands Park where it uprooted 148 trees, tore the roof off a lodge, and blocked a mile of the Bath Road with fallen trees. Hardly a roof or a tree survived at Cherhill where the miller counted fifty fallen elms. Large trees were carried hundreds of yards. The storm continued eastwards to wreak damage at Winterbourne Monkton, Glory Ann and Rockley, and ultimately expire on the Ogbourne Downs.

In 1792 the coach road was re-aligned to a more sheltered route along the lower slopes to the north of Cherhill Down. This re-alignment left the present A4 at the lay-by (076693) half-a-mile west of Beckhampton roundabout and is traceable as it follows an earthwork bank from Knoll Down and over Cherhill Down. At 055697 it followed the banks of a rectangular earthwork enclosure east of White Horse Plantation before swinging south-west around the north edge of Oldbury hillfort, passing above the White Horse and past the Cherhill Monument before resuming its direction westwards past another unnamed beech-capped knoll (044693) and running on to join Green Lanes (027695) and swing north-west into the main road opposite Hayle Farm between Calne and Cherhill.

Beside the coach road on Cherhill Down a mile west of Beckhampton (at 070689) Andrews and Dury on their 1773 map show the gibbet on which were gibbeted the notorious Cherhill gang of highwaymen after they were executed at Devizes.

Beech clump beside Old Bath Road on Knoll Down

About 1826 Sir Goldsworthy Gurney ran an experimental steam carriage on the road from London to Bristol, presumably across Cherhill Down. By 1841 the Great Western Railway had reached Bristol and Bath, and the public quickly transferred its custom from the stagecoaches to the new form of travel. The last stagecoach from Bristol to London ran in 1843. The turnpikes had always been unpopular for both levying tolls and for inflating the costs of local goods by making it possible to transport them out of the district to obtain higher prices. When the Devizes Turnpike Trusts were finally wound up the *Illustrated London News* for 14 November 1868 carried an account of the great celebrations in Devizes which included a procession led by a brass band, a bonfire upon which was burnt some turnpike gates purchased especially for the purpose, and a firework display on Devizes Green attended by an audience of several thousands.

The loss of stagecoach business was catastrophic to the inns along the route of the Bath Road. The Castle Inn at Marlborough closed in 1843 and became part of Marlborough College, but the Waggon and Horses coaching inn at Beckhampton, built in 1669 as The Bear with lands attached for the overnight resting of cattle which were being driven to London, managed to survive. The racing stables and fine Georgian house within the apex of the triangle of downland described in this chapter, situated between the A4 and the A361 at Beckhampton and shown by Andrews and Dury on their 1773 map, had been the Beckhampton Inn, built with stables for coach horses on the Bath Road. It became a racing stable after stagecoaches were superceded by the railway.

Blackland Park

At the opposite extremity of this district, immediately west of these south-west Marlborough downlands, Blackland Park was created around lakes formed on the River Marden as it flows west from Calstone. Blackland is accessible to walkers as a number of public footpaths cross its park. The name 'Blackland' is suggestive of rich earth and of early occupation, perhaps in Roman times, as is the local name Blackland Street, 'street' in country districts almost always indicating a former Roman way. In the context of 'Black' place-names being associated with Roman sites the Roman town in Black Field at *Cunetio* near Marlborough comes to mind. The Roman road crosses the downs north of King's Play Hill and only a mile south of Blackland Park. Between Blackland Park and the Roman road a medieval moated site exists at Blacklands Farm (012686).

This secluded area of unspoilt and flora-rich countryside tucked away in the triangle formed between two very busy roads – the A4 and the A361 west of Beckhampton roundabout – is a delightful area for walking. It is seen at its best on a balmy summer evening when the slanting sunshine enhances the modelling of the chalk downland landscape. The heart of the area lies in the coombes east of Calstone. Having once discovered this comparatively little known area, many walkers will find that it becomes one of their favourite areas and its many attractions will draw them back time and time again.

Beacon Hill from Oliver's Castle

Suggested Walks around Calstone, Oldbury and Roundway Down

5A: From Calstone Wellington over the Eastern Area (10 miles: map 173):

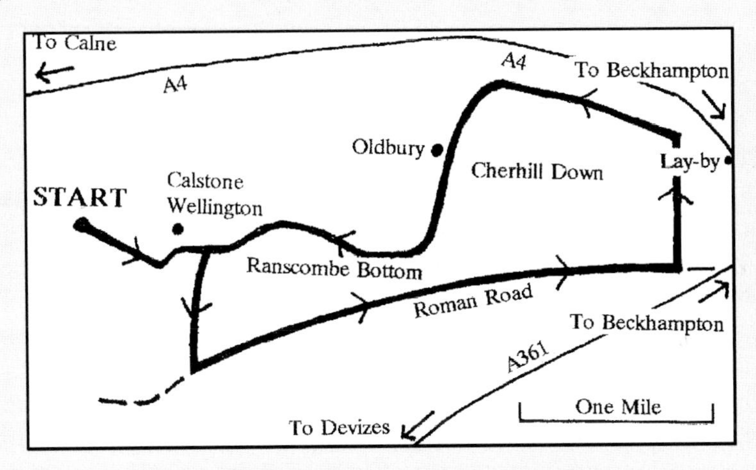

Most of the attractions of the eastern section of the area described in this chapter may be seen by parking at Calstone Wellington where parking is available in the small lay-by on the approach to Calstone from the west or opposite Manor Farm (024684). There is no parking available near South Farm. Walk east through the village and then south from South Farm (030684) to the Roman road on the north flank of Morgan's Hill (030674). The Roman road may then be followed eastwards over North Down to near the A361 at about 071683. From this point the well-preserved agger of the protected continuation of the Roman road may be seen ahead aligned on Silbury Hill. This eastern end of the downs towards Beckhampton is devoted to the exercise of horses from the racing stables on both the turf and all-weather gallops, but at the time of writing (late 1996) the landowner allows free access to the public with the right to roam over the area except when horses are using the gallops. It is therefore permissible to strike north from the Roman road across West Down and cross the delightful secluded coombe under Cherhill Down to the line of the Old Bath Road at the top of the hill west of Knoll Down. The continuation of this walk is west along the line of the former Old Bath Road as far as 055699. At this point change direction, proceed south-west then south over Cherhill Down and, after walking past and perhaps around Oldbury Castle, continue south and then west down the side coombe into Ranscombe Bottom which may then be followed west back to Calstone. This walk, which in its entirety amounts to about 10 miles, may easily be divided it into two walks, one being followed as a shortened walk from Calstone, the other from the lay-by on the A4 (077692) half a mile west of Beckhampton.

5B: From near Oliver's Castle over the Western Area (8 miles; Map 173): The western section of the area is easiest seen by an 8 mile walk, parking near Oliver's Castle (at 004647) and walking south-east down the track to 013639, anti-clockwise round The Plantation, and then north-east across Roundway Hill and the site of the Battle of Roundway Down to the crossing of tracks at 022659. From this crossing follow the track (once the former Old Bath Road) which runs east, across the Bishops Cannings to Calne road to Old Shepherd's Shore on Wansdyke (040666). From here the walk is north-west along Wansdyke over Morgan's Hill, crossing the road again at The Firs (018673) north of the golf course, following the road for a short distance, and then from 015674 turning south and walking past the Hampsley Hollow riding centre (009667) into Heddington village. From Heddington the return to the downs is south-east up the road to Hill Cottage (009656) and through 005654 back to the start point near Oliver's Castle which should not be missed and may be visited by a short diversion at the end or the beginning of the walk.

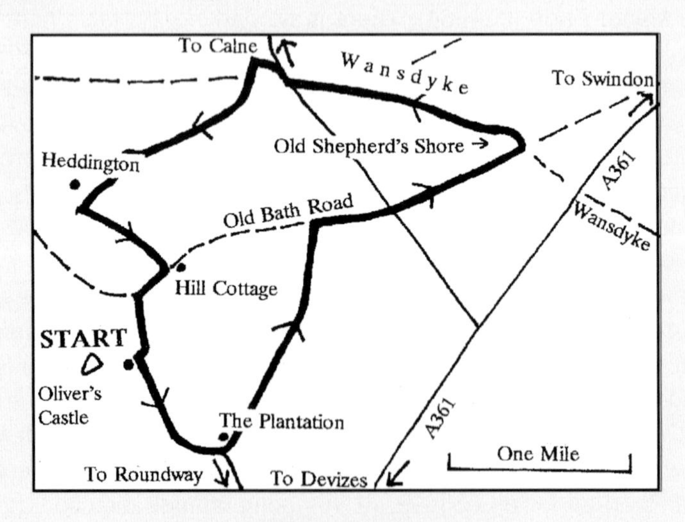

Walks 5B and 5C

5C: From near Oliver's Castle over the site of the Battle of Roundway Down (4 miles: map 173; map on page 136):
The site of the Battle of Roundway Down may be conveniently explored on foot by a shorter walk, parking near Oliver's Castle (at 004647) and walking north and north-east past Hill Cottage (009656) on King's Play Hill to 022659 which was near the centre of the action, then south-west over Roundway Hill to The Plantation at 013641, returning north-west up the track towards Oliver's Castle.

5D: The Western Escarpment from near Roundway Village (4.5 to 6.5 miles: map 173):
The dramatically modelled western escarpment of these downs is overlooked from the north edge of Oliver's Castle, but it is best seen from below, from the scarp foot footpath which runs immediately to its west. After parking in Consciences Lane a little west of Roundway village, from 006634 walk north-west beneath the hanging woods of Roundway Hill Covert, passing Mother Anthony's Well and the west end of the Oliver's Castle promontory of down. A short diversion can be made to view Bloody Ditch. From below Oliver's Castle continue north and follow the footpath round the western shoulder of Beacon Hill. The views from this footpath of the escarpment between Oliver's Castle and Beacon Hill is in my estimation one of the most dramatic sights of Wiltshire. Upon reaching the turnpike (992658) which descends north-west over Beacon Hill, follow the yew and juniper lined old road on to the Roundway plateau. Upon emerging at the top of the hill a footpath can be followed (from 001654) south back to Oliver's Castle, either descending the extremely steep south face of the hill to rejoin the outgoing footpath, or continuing south-east and returning to the starting point through Roundway village. Alternatively the walk may be extended to about 6.5 miles by walking farther east from the top of Beacon Hill past Hill Cottage, at 022659 turning south and crossing the centre of the battle site, and returning through Roundway village.

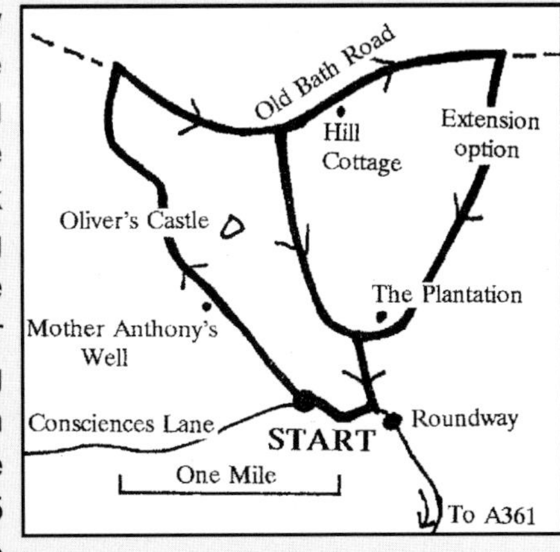

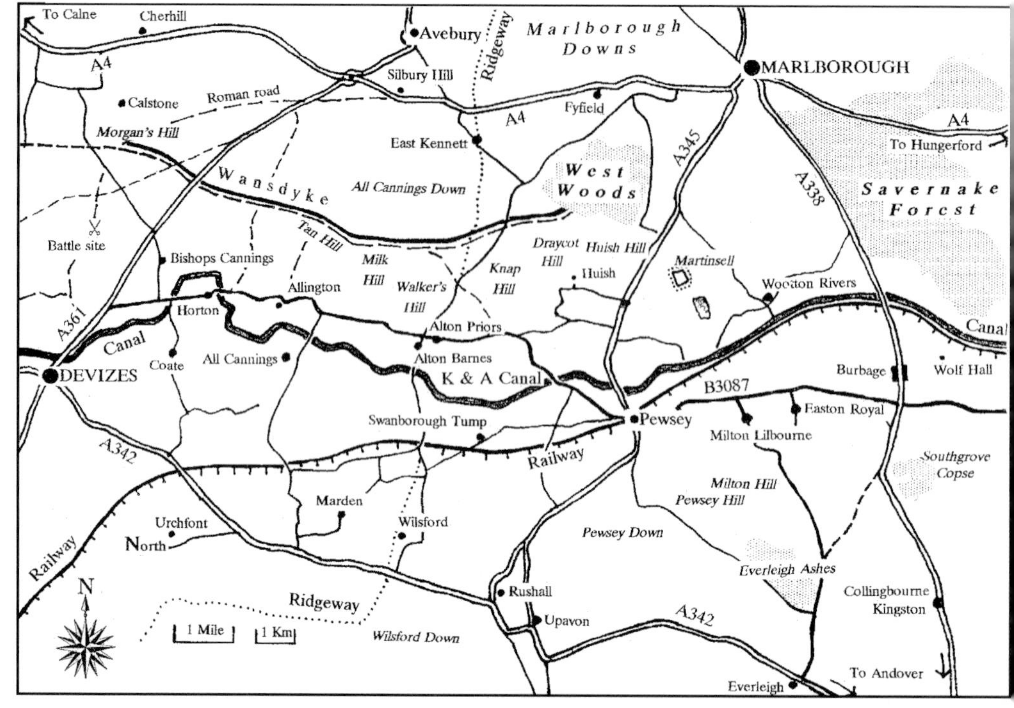

Above: The Vale of Pewsey

Below: The North Escarpment: Huish Hill and Martinsell from foot of Walker's Hill

6 The Vale of Pewsey
including Savernake Forest

(map Landranger 173)

To provide an interlude from the high downlands which have so far formed the principal subjects of this book, this chapter is devoted to one of the finest valleys in Wiltshire. The Vale of Pewsey effectively separates north Wiltshire from south Wiltshire. It also separates the prehistoric centres of Avebury and Stonehenge, and the two great masses of Wiltshire chalk downland – the Marlborough Downs from Salisbury Plain. The valley extends from the area immediately east of Devizes around Bishops Cannings and Etchilhampton where the valley is wide, eastwards past Stanton St Bernard and the two Alton villages to the area immediately east of the large village of Pewsey which is effectively the capital of the Vale and gives it its name. At its east end the Vale of Pewsey merges imperceptibly with the environs of the now much reduced Forest of Savernake.

In the absence of a substantial river, the Vale of Pewsey is in effect a huge, dry, upland coombe. Although no river runs along the length of the Vale, the Salisbury Avon originates in the Vale as a number of minor streams which combine near Puckshipton and Pewsey into two major tributaries which, after their confluence near Upavon, break through the southern chalk escarpment of the Vale to run south along the Valley of the Avon to Salisbury. The precise source of the Avon is uncertain, so much so that Brian Vesey-Fitzgerald in his book on *The Hampshire Avon* (1950) never satisfactorily resolved the problem of its source, even after consulting the Ordnance Survey who told him that the actual source might be 'any one of a number of streams'.

Other springs which rise around Urchfont – 'font' means 'spring' – flow west ultimately to feed the Bristol Avon, and to the north of Pewsey Vale the River Kennet runs parallel to and at a higher level than the Vale of Pewsey but never breaks through into the Vale. Pewsey Vale is therefore unusual in that it is a valley associated with two watersheds, one between the Bristol Avon and the Salisbury Avon, the other being its north escarpment which forms the watershed between the River Kennet and the Salisbury Avon.

Geologically, Pewsey Vale is a valley of mixed Greensand and Gault which separates the two great areas of Wiltshire chalkland, the Greensand of the Vale having been exposed by the weathering away of the chalk which formerly overlaid it. Its geology is in fact far more involved but, greatly simplified, the Vale consists of a mixture of Greensands and Gault clays with drifted deposits overlying them in which over the years its farmers have maintained fertility by practising sound husbandry.

Picked Hill and Woodborough Hill remain as isolated columns of chalk which have survived as outliers rising from the valley floor. Greensand tends to hold water and some parts of the Vale of Pewsey are marshy, especially towards Pewsey where the 'ey' element ('eyot' is an old name for an island) and the fact that Pewsey was sometimes known as 'Pewsedge' confirm that the village is surrounded by marshy ground. The west end of the Vale around All Cannings is similarly marshy and was mentioned as *Caningan Mœrse* ('Cannings Marsh') in the *Anglo-Saxon Chronicle* under the year 1010 in connection with a Viking raid down the Ridgeway into the valley.

Unlike the Kennet Valley to its north, which is followed by the A4, the Vale of Pewsey has from the walker's point of view the advantage of containing only minor roads, one a delightful little-used road along the valley floor from Devizes through the Alton villages to Pewsey, the other the busier A342 Lydeway which runs along the southern edge of the valley from Devizes to Andover. Several other roads run north to south across the Vale of Pewsey. The minor road from Lockeridge to the Altons follows the Ridgeway in its crossing of the col between Walker's Hill and Knap Hill to descend into and cross the valley. Further to the east the A345 Marlborough-Salisbury road runs south from Marlborough and crosses the Vale through Oare and Pewsey.

The Escarpments of the Vale

The dominant natural landscape features of the Vale of Pewsey are the escarpments which define its northern and southern limits. The great northern escarpment consists from west to east of Easton Hill, Tan Hill and Milk Hill – the last two being at 964 feet (294m) the highest hills in Wiltshire – Walker's Hill, Knap Hill, Golden Ball Hill, Draycot Hill, and Huish Hill. The range ends with the great bluff of Martinsell. These hills are a kind shared territory, for they form both the south edge of the Marlborough Downs and the north escarpment of the Vale of Pewsey. The southern escarpment of the Vale is similarly shared with Salisbury Plain.

H.J. Massingham wrote of the northern escarpment as being:

> the long line and masterly modelling in col, headland and saddleback

> of the Marlborough Downs ... the long barrow of Adam's Grave forms one slope of a green conical mound and below it the land falls away to a wide terrace supported by flying buttresses on two sides,

and Desmond Hawkins wrote of this escarpment that it 'must be counted one of the most memorable sights that Wiltshire can offer'.

Several features of interest occur along the top of this escarpment. A little behind it runs the great linear earthwork of Wansdyke and some of these features have already been described in Chapter 2 on the Wansdyke countryside. The Alton White Horse which has been cut in the south face of the indent between Milk Hill and Walker's Hill (106637) is a prominent feature of the escarpment seen from the valley. It was cut at the instigation of a local farmer called Mr Pile who commissioned an itinerant artist to create the figure.

Knap Hill (left) and Giant's Grave.

This northern escarpment of Pewsey Vale around Knap Hill was formerly used for rabbit warrening – that is the farming of rabbits for meat and fur. One of the mounds beside the Workway Drove under Knap Hill (at 116637) was a pillow-mound, although it has been marked as one of a group of tumuli by the Ordnance Survey. Pillow-mounds are man-made low oblong mounds – hence their name – now generally recognised to have been constructed for rabbits to burrow into. They date from betwen the time that the Normans introduced rabbits into England in the 12th century, through the medieval period to the 18th century. It is possible that the former residents of the now deserted village of Shaw (see Chapter 3) in its remote downland situation a mile and a half north of the Workway Drove were responsible for managing these rabbit warrens.

From the Greensand floor of the Vale rise two prominent isolated chalk hills which are features of the landscape from most viewpoints in the Vale of Pewsey. These are Woodborough Hill (118613) with its top-knot of trees, and Picked Hill (124612), a conical hill which obtains its name from the same source as pick, a pointed implement. The former hill may be approached along a footpath from the canal towpath, but Picked Hill is not accessible by public footpath.

The southern escarpment of Pewsey Vale is fine but undoubtedly less fine than the northern which is both steeper and more dramatically modelled and scalloped. Along the southern hills above the Vale of Pewsey the Ridgeway swings west after crossing the valley and follows the north scarp of Salisbury Plain from east to west over Wilsford Hill, Redhorn Hill – with between them the delightfully named Marden Cowbag (090555) and Chirton Maggot (068552) – and Urchfont Hill. East of the point where the Ridgeway climbs Wilsford Hill the escarpment, after dipping to allow the Salisbury Avon to pierce it at Upavon, is formed by Upavon Hill and Milton Hill. Excellent panoramic views of the entire range of hills which form the north escarpment of the Vale of Pewsey are obtained from several points on this southern escarpment.

William Cobbett enthused over the Vale of Pewsey when he first saw it from Milton Hill on this southern escarpment above Milton Lilbourne on his *Rural Rides* in 1826:

> The shepherd showed me the way towards Milton [Lilbourne]; and at the end of about a mile, from the top of a very high part of the down, with a steep slope towards the valley, I first saw this Valley of the Avon [actually Pewsey Vale]; and a most beautiful sight it was! Great as my expectations have been, they were more than fulfilled. I delight in this sort of country: I sat upon my horse and looked over Milton, Easton [Royal] and Pewsey for half an hour, though I had not breakfasted.

Milton Hill above Milton Lilbourne, from which Cobbett first saw the Vale of Pewsey.

It was a rare compliment to the scenery of the Pewsey Vale for the ample and irascible William Cobbett to gaze upon it for half an hour before he took his breakfast!

Milton Hill offers the best walking on the south side of the Vale of Pewsey. It is accessible from the droveway which runs north-east from Pewsey to Everleigh at Down Farm (184569), or from the other end of the droveway at 202590 near Easton Clump (211593). This point is accessible by car south from Milton Lilbourne. The walking on Milton Hill is splendid, with fine views from the gigantic Neolithic long barrow of Giant's Grave (189582) looking north across the Vale to Martinsell. From Giant's Grave its namesake is visible (at 166632) four miles to the north on the west promontory of Martinsell, as well as Adam's Grave (113633), the most dramatically sited long barrow in Wiltshire six miles to the north-west on Walker's Hill. On Pewsey Hill west of the Giant's Grave the Pewsey White Horse is a modern creation cut in 1937 to replace an earlier White Horse.

The Vale of Pewsey is now marred by two lines of electricity pylons. Ancient men, who lived in close association with their landscapes, seem instinctively to have enhanced the countryside with their works which appear to have grown naturally out of the landscape, as evidenced by the gloriously sited

Adam's Grave long barrow which adds so much to the impact Walker's Hill above Alton Barnes, and Giant's Grave which positively embellishes the western promontory of Martinsell. The facility with which ancient men by their actions instinctively enhanced the landscape must be explained by the fact that they lived close to nature and venerated the landscape in which they lived. This attitude survived into Victorian times, but today most people have grown remote from all natural things and the pressures arising from a much increased population and that population's wish to travel has led society to exploit the landscape to provide people with subsistence for a higher standard of living and satisfy the demands of the motor car which has become the principal means of travelling.

Today we seem to have lost the instinct for improving the landscape by our activities in the countryside and, although the canal and the railway were successfully integrated into Pewsey Vale in the 19th century, the most noticeable 20th century additions to the landscape of the Vale are these monstrous electricity pylons. As early as 1928 the architect Clough William Ellis – who incidentally designed the extensions to Oare House – anticipated the dangers posed by electrification undertaken by the National Grid and warned of possible severe shocks to amenity, but his warning was not heeded and as a consequence today and for the foreseeable future the Vale of Pewsey will suffer from the existence of these intrusive pylons. The most objectionable line runs assertively below the southern escarpment of Pewsey Vale past Urchfont and Wedhampton, the other past Bishops Cannings and through Beechingstoke and the two Manningford villages. They combine and accompany each other eastwards under Milton Hill. How Cobbett would have fulminated against these 20th century intrusions into his 'land of promise'.

It is to be hoped that in this age of increasing exploitation and desecration of the countryside the imminent dangers to the Wiltshire downland landscapes posed by the introduction on high ground of wind turbines to generate electricity will not come about and prove to be a similar long-term disaster.

The Canal and the Railway

The potential of the Vale of Pewsey as a convenient route to the west was recognised when the promoters of the Kennet and Avon Canal and the directors of the Great Western Railway adopted it for the routes of the canal and the railway, both 19th century introductions which could have been intrusions into the Vale but are in fact well integrated into the landscape. They enter the Vale close together at its east end near Wootton Rivers, but by the time they reach Pewsey they have diverged to half a mile apart, with the canal lying nearer the northern escarpment of the Vale. As they continue westwards they progressively diverge until they pass either side of Etchilhampton, the canal being two miles to its north and the railway a mile to its south. The canal then continues west to Devizes and descends Caen Hill beside the A361 by a dramatic flight of locks which are worth going a long way to see, while the railway swings south-west to pass two miles south-east of Potterne, its former line to Devizes having now closed.

Canal and Alton White Horse

The Second World War

The many derelict brick pillboxes that are to be seen beside the Kennet and Avon Canal throughout the Vale of Pewsey, particularly around the Alton villages, are survivals from the Second World War. In 1940 it was decided that a three hundred mile line of defence against German invasion should be formed across southern England to defend London and the manufacturing areas of the Midlands by reinforcing natural obstacles against tanks by the construction of pillboxes. The Kennet and Avon Canal formed part of that line right across Wiltshire. The pillboxes that were built were a mixture of infantry machine-gun pattern and anti-tank pillboxes. The former predominated because most of our anti-tank guns had been abandoned at Dunkirk. It is not generally realised that this defensive line, which was constructed by order of the C-in-C Home Forces General Sir William Ironside, was officially regarded as obsolete as soon as it was completed. It was built at great expense and effort over two months in the early summer of 1940 but when General Ironside retired in July 1940 and was replaced by General Alan Brooke, who had experience of fighting against German panzer tanks, the latter commented on these defensive measures in his diary three days after being appointed : 'The static rear line did not fall in with my conception.

To my mind our defence should be of a far more mobile and offensive nature'.

Another association of the Vale of Pewsey with the Second World War is contained in the paintings of Paul Nash (1889-1946) who first became interested in this part of Wiltshire in 1933 when he discovered the standing stones of Avebury which he described as wonderful and disquieting'. At that time he wrote: 'If anything will preserve my interest in landscape from a painter's point of view it will be this country'. When he was official war artist to the Air Ministry Nash produced about a dozen watercolour paintings of shot-down German aircraft which include as backgrounds landscapes which Nash knew and loved. One of these paintings ('Death of a Dragon') illustrates a burning German bomber in a field with three distinctive rounded hills in the background which bear a very strong resemblance to the north escarpment of Pewsey Vale. Nash habitually used photographs as the basis for his paintings and it is interesting to speculate whether he used a photograph of the Vale of Pewsey for the background to this painting. Another of his paintings ('Encounter in the Afternoon') shows a Messerschmidt down in a field beside a steep strictly geometrical conical hill that can only be Silbury Hill. It may be significant that both of these paintings were produced at the same period, in 1940.

Pewsey Vale contains a much greater concentration of villages than either the Marlborough Downs to its north or Salisbury Plain to its south. The twin villages of Alton Priors and Alton Barnes which stand at the very heart of the Vale at the crossing of minor roads south of Walker's Hill are well worth incorporating in walks. Alton Barnes has a fine Anglo-Saxon church with the long-and-short quoins (corner stones) which are typical of that period, while the redundant medieval church at Alton Priors contains an Elizabethan monument to Sir William Button, an ancestor of the friend of the same name of the Wiltshire writer and antiquary John Aubrey. A succession of Sir William Buttons owned much land in this area including an estate at Shaw beside Wansdyke near West Woods (see Chapter 3), until a daughter took their lands by marriage to Clementine Walker who gave his name to Walker's Hill.

A short distance south of the two Alton villages is Honey Street (102616), a canalside hamlet which came into existence when the canal was constructed and was described by Sir Nikolaus Pevsner as 'A minor, but the best, bit of canal scenery in Wiltshire'. Here is found The Barge Inn, a canalside pub which can provide refreshment on walks.

Situated in a field south of Honey Street called Hanging Stone Hurst, west of Hurst's Farm and beside a footpath, is the isolated standing sarsen stone known as the Hanging Stone (099604). Local folklore records that a

Above: Alton Barnes church. The house was formerly the home of the glass engraver Laurence Whistler;

Left: One of three memorial panes by Laurence Whistler in Alton Barnes church, this one to the farmer Arthur Guy Stratton.

man who had stolen a sheep and slung it round his neck rested against this stone, placing the sheep on the stone. The sheep then slipped off the stone on the opposite side to the man, tightened the rope, and hanged him. The story is not unique to this area for there are 'Hangmen's Stones' with similar legends attached in many counties. This stone was probably set up as a boundary marker, being now within a hundred yards of a parish boundary.

The village of Easton Royal, situated below and a little east of Milton Hill, derives the second element of its name from the fact that it was formerly in the Royal Forest of Savernake. In the Vale of Pewsey the second element of many of the two element place-names are frequently dropped for convenience, so that Easton Royal becomes Easton and Milton Lilbourne is generally Milton. South of Easton more fine downland walking is available around Easton Hill and Clump by taking a four mile walk south-east on to the downs passing Crowdown Clump (217577) – formerly known as Godsbury – continuing to Aughton Down, turning back, and returning down the track which runs round the west side of Easton Hill to Easton Royal.

The Marshlands of the Vale

In the flat marshy west end of Pewsey Vale around All Cannings there is good level walking around one of the sources of the Salisbury Avon at Etchilhampton Water east of Etchilhampton village. H.W. Timperley devoted an entire chapter of his *The Vale of Pewsey* to 'Curlew on Cannings Marsh', describing the walking in the marshy area around All Cannings, Etchilhampton and Patney, and particularly along the lane which leaves the Etchilhampton to All Cannings road at Heath Knapp (059604) where curlew are still heard. This lane, which he describes as having been originally 'one of the few comparatively firm ways across the ancient marsh', takes the walker south past Hatfield Farm and across the railway line towards the Lydeway near Wedhampton. The return may be by way of the villages of Charlton and Patney

The track south from Allington across the canal (at 067626) to the church at All Cannings was known as the Corpse Road because the dead of Allington had to be carried along it for burial at All Cannings.

Samuel Taylor Coleridge (1772-1834), the friend of Wordsworth and author of the *Lyrical Ballads* (1798) which included 'The Rime of the Ancient Mariner', had several connections with Wiltshire. For a time he lived with a lawyer friend called Morgan at Calne, and he knew All Cannings from visiting his friend its rector, the Reverend J.A. Methuen.

Four miles south-east of All Cannings more valley walking is available through the water-meadows (098576) which lie to the north-west of Wilsford. These are crossed by the line of the former Ridgeway running south from Broad Street (106591) past the ancient settlement of Puckshipton (the name is derived from 'puck' and 'shippen', meaning 'goblin's cattle shed') to Wilsford. The return route to Broad Street from Wilsford may be by one of several footpaths past Cuttenham Farm (107571) with its ford – now a road bridge – mentioned in a Saxon charter.

Whilst in this part of Pewsey Vale a worthwhile visit (perhaps before or after a walk) is to Marden Earthwork, a little north-east of Marden village and west of Puckshipton. Although little of it now survives, Marden Henge was the largest 'henge' monument so far identified in Britain, larger that either Avebury or Stonehenge. It enclosed 35 acres in a loop of the River Avon and included within it an immense mound known as Hatfield Barrow, claimed to have been 200 feet (61m) in diameter and well over 20 feet (6m) high when Colt Hoare excavated it in 1807. It has since been ploughed down. If the claim for its size are correct, this was the third largest man-made mound in Britain, exceeded only by Silbury seven miles to its north and Marlborough Mount ten miles to its north-east. All were perhaps significantly situated beside rivers and were constructed at a time when river worship was usual. That Hatfield Barrow was not a barrow at all is suggested by the fact that no interment was found in it by Colt Hoare who, despite describing it as a 'gigantic tumulus', suspected a non-sepulchral purpose as the reason for the construction of this mound.

Wilsford is a charming linear village consisting of many cottages, a church, and a farm at each end of the village. The cottages, in varied styles and materials and generally under thatch, are fine examples of vernacular building. Both its farms – Wilsford House to the west and Cuttenham Farm to the east of Wilsford – are fine brick buildings, particularly the latter for which I have a special admiration as an example of fine restrained building reposing sedately in its landscape.

A little east of Wilsford, and like Wilsford sitting discreetly a little aside from the A342 Devizes to Andover road, is the village of Charlton which was described by Timperley as 'a small, mellow-toned place of brick, timber and thatch'. Charlton was the home of the rustic poet Stephen Duck whose career will be related later in this chapter.

In the fine Norman church at the east end of Pewsey Vale at Manningford Bruce is a memorial tablet to Mary Nicholas, died 1686, who as Mary Lane together with her sister assisted Charles II in his escape after his defeat at the Battle of Worcester in his attempt to regain his father's throne during the Commonwealth in 1651.

Savernake Forest and West Woods

Savernake and West Woods, the latter having once been part of the former, offer options for woodland walking associated with the Vale of Pewsey. Savernake is very popular and has been very highly esteemed by writers including Richard Jefferies and W.H. Hudson. These writers wrote at a time that had not experienced the impact of the motor car from which in my view Savernake suffers severely, having a private motor road through its centre. My own preference is for West Woods which are much more secluded and are criss-crossed by several footpaths. In spring they are carpeted with bluebells and bluebell 'forays' are organised. On these days West Woods are best avoided.

Care should be taken when walking in Savernake Forest, or in any other extensive woodland, for distant landmarks are screened by the trees and it is easy to become disorientated and lost. On several occasions I have discovered bemused walkers wandering utterly lost in Savernake, and in October 1996 tragedy struck when an eighty-five year old man became lost in Savernake for several days, suffered severely from exposure, and ultimately died. When walking in extensive woodland, especially on sunless days, it is advisable for even experienced walkers to carry a compass which will enable them to walk a straight line to find the edge of the woods. More woodland walking is available associated with Pewsey Vale in the woods of Everleigh Ashes (195565) south of Milton Hill.

W.H. Hudson (1841-1922), a writer who will be discussed later in connection with The Wylye Valley (Chapter 8 of Volume 2) and Great Ridge Wood (Chapter 10), also knew the Vale of Pewsey and Savernake Forest. In *A Traveller in Little Things* (1923) he wrote a chapter headed 'A Wiltshire Village' devoted to a stay he made in the village of Burbage, at the east end of Pewsey Vale and a few miles south of Savernake Forest near Easton Royal. Hudson was intrigued by the way in which the cottages of Burbage are perched on banks high above the street through the village.

A mile east of Burbage and towards the east end of Pewsey Vale stands the now much reduced Wolf Hall, formerly the home of the hereditary wardens of Savernake. We have seen in Chapter 2 (page 71) how the Seymours, comparatively late arrivals from St Maur in Normandy, acquired by marriage into the Esturmeys the Wardenship and thus secured their future. It was at Wolf Hall that Jane Seymour in 1536 caught the eye of Henry VIII, who was in Wiltshire for the hunting, and very rapidly succeeded the executed Anne Boleyn as his third wife. Jane provided Henry with the son who was desperately needed to secure the succession, but died shortly after the birth. After Henry died in 1547 Jane's son succeeded as Edward VI at the age of ten, his uncle Edward Seymour effectively reigning as Lord Protector Somerset until in 1552 he was conspired against and executed. The young King Edward noted unfeelingly in his diary: 'Somerset had his head cut off', but he too died in 1553 and was succeeded first by his Catholic sister Mary and then by Anne Boleyn's daughter Elizabeth I.

Today practically nothing of the former Seymour mansion at Wolf Hall survives for it was replaced as the home of the Wardens of Savernake by Tottenham House two miles to its north at the south end of the present much reduced forest. At the time of his death Protector Somerset was constructing a substantial mansion more fitting his exalted position in Bedwyn Brail (284625), a wood three miles east of Wolf Hall, but with his death the work was abandoned.

Wolf Hall is passed by a very minor public road, and Bedwyn Brail is crossed north to south by a public footpath which runs south from Great Bedwyn. The unusual name 'Brail', which is applied to several woods and to Brail Farm in this area, derives from 'Broyle', an old forest name for an enclosed wood stocked with deer.

Great Bedwyn church, which stands beside the canal three miles north of Wolf Hall, is a repository of fine monuments including one to Sir John Seymour (died 1536), the father of Jane Seymour and Protector Somerset. Sir John's body was removed to Great Bedwyn in 1590 from Easton Royal church which was the former burial place of the Seymours.

A mile north of Great Bedwyn is one of the most moving and least-known buildings of Wiltshire. Standing in the farmyard of Manor Farm and on the ramparts of Chisbury Iron Age hillfort is the tiny ruined flint and thatched Chapel of St Martin, now used as a barn. This poignant little abandoned building of the late-13th century is full of that elusive atmosphere generated by ruins. It was painted by John Piper (1903-92) who as a boy knew Wiltshire and became a member of the Wiltshire Archaeological Society. He later collaborated in the writing of *The Shell Guide to Wiltshire* (1968). Although not obviously accessible, St Martin's Chapel may be approached up the drive from Chisbury Lane to its north-east. It should on no account be missed by anyone walking in this area.

Wansdyke in West Woods, here much diminished, looking west.

Swanborough Tump

Land in the Vale of Pewsey was owned by Alfred, the future king and saviour of Wessex. By a land charter dated 822 Alfred granted an estate at North Newnton to Aethelhelm, the ealdorman of Wiltshire. Between Pewsey and Woodborough, in the Vale of Pewsey a little south of Cocklebury Farm is Swanborough Tump (132601), formerly a place of importance as the meeting place or 'moot' of the Swanborough Hundred in Anglo-Saxon times. It was recorded as *Swanabeorh* in 987 AD. The name means barrow of the peasants (swains) but it it became known by the local people as Swanborough Ashes from the ash trees which once grew on the mound. This name is confirmed by a document of 1764 which refers to a Court Leet to be held at 'Swanborough Ash'.

This Saxon 'moot' remained the hundred meeting place until the 18th century, but subsequently the location of Swanborough Tump was lost until 1890 when the Rev. H.G. Tomkins identified it. Consequently it is not marked on the early editions of the Ordnance Survey nor – despite the 1764 reference quoted above – on the map published by Andrews and Dury in 1773. The site is now an insignificant low mound trodden almost flat by cattle but still marked by a plaque on a post. It is now named on the current Ordnance Survey maps. Here in the late 9th century, when Wessex was being assailed by the Danes, King Ethelred and his brother Alfred summoned their Council to decide how best the Danish onslaught should be resisted. As a result of this meeting Alfred's will was drawn up to include the agreement which had been reached between himself and Ethelred:

> But it came to pass that we were all harassed with the heathen invasion; then we discussed our childrens' future – how they would need some maintenance, whatever might happen to us through these disasters. When we were assembled at Swanborough we agreed, with the cognizance of the West Saxon Council, that whichever survived the other was to give the other's children the lands which we ourselves acquired and the lands which King Ethelwulf gave us.

Ladies' Bridge

A few hundred yards to the north of Swanborough Tump the Kennet and Avon Canal is bridged near Cocklebury Farm by Ladies' Bridge (129606). Although merely an accommodation bridge, Ladies' Bridge differs from all the other canal bridges by being very ornate and built of stone rather than the usual brick. This is believed to be because Mrs Susanna Wroughton, who owned Wilcot Manor when the canal was built, made the building of a decorative bridge and the widening of the canal to its east into Wide Water a condition of the sale of the land to the canal company. The single flattish arch displays much vermiculated rustication, swags, patterned panels and medallions, together with balustraded parapets. Pevsner was told that Ladies' Bridge was designed by Rennie, the engineer in charge of the Kennet and Avon Canal construction. Ladies Bridge is said to be haunted by a ghostly lady.

Wilcot is a delightful village which in 1624 is alleged to have been plagued by an incessant inexplicable ringing of its church bells. This was so persistent that James I, who was intensely interested in the supernatural, sent down his investigator to report on the phenomenon. Walkers in the Wilcot area should note that Cocklebury Lane which runs past Wilcot Manor to Cocklebury was described by Brian Vesey-Fitzgerald in *The Hampshire Avon* (1950) as being 'in wet weather the muddiest lane in England'.

The Canal at Wide Water, from Ladies Bridge.

Some of the walks over the north escarpment of the Vale have already been described in Chapter 3 on the Wansdyke countryside when following the Ridgeway south over Wansdyke and between Walker's Hill and Knap Hill. Between these hills is the car park on the Workway Drove (116637) under Knap Hill which provides a good starting point for many walks. Workway is derived from the Saxon *weorc-weg*, meaning 'the way by the stronghold', the stronghold being Knap Hill which is a Neolithic causewayed

Maria Hare at Alton Barnes

The quality of the walking and the way in which the Vale of Pewsey insidiously takes a hold of its walkers is reflected in the writings of Maria Hare who came to Alton Barnes with her husband the Reverend Augustus Hare when they married in 1829. In a letter dated 15th October 1829 during her first week at the rectory Maria recorded her first experiences of walking in the Vale:

> We took an exploring walk, and after wading through a bed of mortar we did try to get to a dry walk up the downs. Our great object is always where to find a place tolerably dry for our walks, and our first errand to Devizes has been to beg a shoemaker to come and measure us for waterproof shoes.

Prospective walkers should not be deterred by this adverse account of walking in Pewsey Vale because soon Maria Hare was writing in very different vein:

> I had such a delightful ramble over the Downs ; the sun shone so bright, and the air was clear and reviving, and I pushed on till I turned a point of the hill, and there sprawling beneath me lay the great White Horse in all its chalky glory.

camp with its surrounding ditches bridged by causeways making it indefensible. These causewayed camps – Rybury on Clifford's Hill is another example – are now believed to have been places of assembly, probably used as the sites for feasts in the autumn when most cattle were killed because there was insufficient feed to maintain them over the winter.

The towpath of the Kennet and Avon Canal provides continuous linear walking along the Vale but the walking is inevitably flat and rather monotonous. The towpath is best walked in short lengths and incorporated in walks on to the surrounding downland areas to provide the variety of some waterside walking on walks which are principally over the adjoining downlands.

Edward Thomas and Pewsey Vale

The enthusiastic long-distance walker Edward Thomas described his wanderings in the Vale of Pewsey in his longest and favourite poem 'Lob' which begins:

At hawthorn-time in Wiltshire travelling
In search of something chance would never bring ...

Soon the poet is listing a litany of Pewsey Vale place-names :

There were three Manningfords, – Abbots, Bohun and Bruce:
And whether Alton, not Manningford, it was
My memory could not decide, because
There were both Alton Barnes and Alton Priors.
All had their churches, graveyards, farms and byres,
Lurking to one side up the paths and lanes,
Seldom well seen except by aeroplanes.

Later in 'Lob' Thomas mentions the Alton Barnes White Horse, Walker's Hill, and Adam's Grave, which he refers to by its local name of 'Adam's Point'.

Huish

In addition to providing a good starting point for walks, the tiny village of Huish also has its ghost story which was written-up by Charles Dickens as 'The Ghost of Pit Pond' in *Household Words* in 1867. Pit Pond is the pond south of Huish Farm and church. It was, within my recollection, much more a rustic village pond. It has now suffered from being tidied up and its entire character has been lost.

The story tells of a young bachelor farmer called Reeves of Huish Farm; the farming family of Reeves were ancestors of the Wiltshire writer Richard Jefferies. One evening a horse ran away with its girl rider down Huish Hill and was stopped by Farmer Reeves who invited the young lady into Huish Farm to recover. The outcome was that Mr Reeves fell in love with her but his feelings were not reciprocated. After she went away he mooned about for a while and then followed the girl, who turned out to be an equestrian circus performer, abroad. Having found that she had died in poverty in Brussels, he returned home in despair, and hanged himself in his barn. His ghost was said to haunt the area of his farm until it was exorcised, particularly the

Stephen Duck

In the chapter headed 'Three Wessex Poets' of his travel book *In Pursuit of Spring* (1914) Edward Thomas wrote of a poet who was born and brought up towards the east end of the Vale of Pewsey, at Charlton. Stephen Duck (1705-1756) was raised as a labourer but, encouraged by the local vicar, studied poetry and aspired to be a poet. His 'The Thresher's Labour' attracted the attention of Queen Caroline who patronised Duck and provided him with sinecure appointments, one of them appropriately as the keeper of Duck Island in St James's Park. Duck took holy orders but, unable to cope with the very highest society in which he circulated, drowned himself in the Kennet at Reading in 1756.

His poetry is not good, but it has an undoubted rustic charm when he was writing of the rural matters which he understood, as in 'The Thresher's Labour', but he was out of his depth when he attempted to emulate the clergymen poets of the time by writing on classical subjects. The late Ralph Whitlock once aptly described Stephen Duck in high society as being 'like a duck out of water'. The Charlton Cat public house at Charlton – a pub which presumably obtained its unusual name from the leopard rampant in the heraldic arms of the Poore family who were lords of Rushall, the pub having formerly been The Poore's Arms – holds an annual 'Duck Feast' in June to commemorate the poet.

area around Pit Pond. The story seems to have been 'borrowed' by Dickens, who loved a ghost story, from the version written by Dudley Costello in the *Piccadilly Annual* for 1848.

In the churchyard at Huish is buried Primula, the first wife of the actor David Niven.

Nature Reserves

Two contrasting nature reserves exist associated with the Vale of Pewsey. A large area of unimproved (that is never ploughed) chalk downland around Walker's Hill and Knap Hill has been designated the Pewsey Downs National Nature Reserve. Around the Pewsey and Woodborough area there are many small wetlands which have often become overgrown with willow and alder. One area of former water-meadows immediately north-west of Pewsey and south of the canal has been preserved as Jone's Mill Nature Reserve. It is managed by the Wiltshire Trust for Nature Conservation and includes a lake dedicated to the memory of Ida Gandy (1885-1977), the daughter of the eccentric Rev. C.W. Hony of Bishops Cannings. Mrs Gandy wrote the histories of Bishops Cannings and Aldbourne parishes.

Martinsell

Of all the hills of Wiltshire, and I have an affection for many, Martinsell at the east end of the northern escarpment of Pewsey Vale is in my estimation the finest. All walkers in Wiltshire should at some time venture on to Martinsell Hill, that great bastion of a hill which is a familiar landmark for half the county of Wiltshire, being visible from above Shrewton sixteen miles away in south Wiltshire, and from Barbury Castle, Hackpen Hill, and Round Hill Downs to the north. Martinsell has fascinated a succession of writers on Wiltshire landscape. H.J. Massingham wrote in *English Downland* (1936): 'Martinsell spells Wiltshire', and 'Never did hill throw out so bold and soaring a bluff as Martinsell over the valley', and in 1954 H.W. Timperley devoted an entire chapter to Martinsell in *The Vale of Pewsey*. Anthony Blunt, the Keeper of the Queen's Pictures who was found to have spied for Russia, directed that his ashes be scattered on Martinsell which he must have known and loved from his boyhood days at Marlborough College. More recently John Chandler has much to say about Giant's Grave and Martinsell in *The Vale of Pewsey* (1991), and the many attractions of Martinsell Hill are also discussed in my own *The Marlborough Downs* (1993).

Giant's Grave, Martinsell, from Huish churchyard.

The unusual name of Martinsell evolved from *Mattelsore* in 1257 through *Matteleshora* in 1370, the final element of the name being from *ora* meaning bank or slope, from which the village of Oare also derives its name. In a charter of about AD 940 Martinsell was *Maetelmes burh*, and Charles Dickens referred to Martinsell in *Household Words* (1867) as Martin's Hill when he gave the following dialogue to a shepherd: 'They do say them that's out at sea,

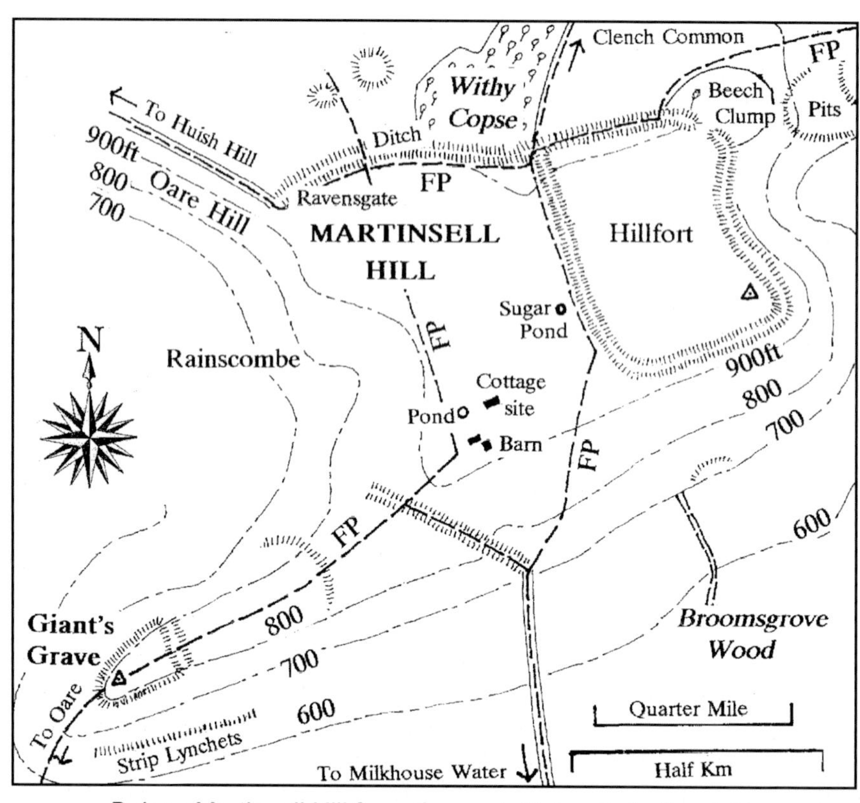

Below: Martinsell Hill from the east. Note pits to the right.

mariners and suchlike, can see the very place we're standin' on ; leastways the white house yon, top of Martin's Hill where the soldiers' graves are'.

The east end of Martinsell is crowned by an Iron Age hillfort enclosing about 32 acres at an altitude of 948 feet (289m) within a roughly rectangular perimeter of single bank and ditch which are of a slight scale suggesting that Martinsell was perhaps merely a cattle enclosure rather than a true hillfort. The only apparent original entrance is at the north-east corner. A number of saucer-shaped pits dug into the eastern slopes of Martinsell (179642) outside the entrance of the hillfort have interested archaeologists. They were for long presumed to be the remains of the hut dwellings of an outguard and were marked 'Pit Dwellings' on the maps, but they are probably merely the eroded remainsof excavations for chalk or flint and are no longer shown as 'Pit Dwellings' by the Ordnance Survey.

From the north-west corner of Martinsell hillfort a linear ditch and traffic way runs west to the large settlement on Huish Hill. Beside it in Withy Copse is located an Iron Age-Romano British rubbish pit or 'midden' that yielded a great deal of pottery and domestic rubbish when it was excavated earlier this century by Mrs Maud Cunnington.

To the west of the hillfort the Martinsell plateau slopes gently to a steep and narrow spur of down which was fortified in the Iron Age as a promontory fort by the construction of a strong bank and ditch across the neck of the down. This promontory became known as the Giant's Grave and a legend arose that if you ran seven times around it the giant would emerge. Potsherds found on Martinsell suggest that Giant's Grave was first settled and that later there was an expansion eastwards on to the more extensive area of Martinsell as the need for greater space arose.

The 'Summer House' shown on Giant's Grave by Andrews and Dury on their 1773 map of Wiltshire was in 1806 mentioned by the archaeologist Colt Hoare when he wrote in a letter: 'From the Summer House observe the finest view in Wiltshire'. Giant's Grave overlooks to its north the great horseshoe hollow of Rainscombe (or 'Ravenscombe'), with the superbly sited Rainscombe House situated at the bottom of the coombe, almost encircled by the heights of Oare Hill, the west end of Martinsell, and Giant's Grave.

Fairs used to be held on Martinsell but were discontinued in 1860, and on Palm Sunday the villagers of Wootton Rivers used to resort to the hill for sports which included sliding down the steep east flank of the hill on jaw bones of horses. It was presumably down this eastern side of Martinsell that George Carter, regarded as one of the finest huntsmen who ever lived and the huntsman to the eccentric Assheton Smith the celebrated master of the Tidworth Hunt, achieved fame by riding his horse and leading his hounds down the steepest slopes of Martinsell.

Until well into the present century a shepherd lived in a cottage (at 173637) near the now ruined flint and brick banded barn (173636) between the hillfort and Giant's Grave. The cottage is now gone (it was near the pond on the summit) as is most of the barn, which I can remember as a substantial building before it was eroded away by neglect and exposure. The last shepherd – Harry Pinchin, I believe – boasted of living in the highest house in Wiltshire and considered it to be 'as healthy a place to live as you could wish'.

On Martinsell Hill the chalk is overlaid by a capping of loamy reddish clay-with-flints in which arable crops are grown. The hill is very exposed and on its summit it is almost always windy, a fact which led Dean Farrar, the master of Marlborough College, to recall 'the natural amphitheatre of Martinsell, and the glorious expanse on which I had gazed so often from its green and breezy summit'. The south ramparts of the hillfort are lined with derelict Scots pine, killed and flayed of their bark by exposure, and the beeches on the eastern ramparts are deformed and stunted by their lesser exposure away from the prevailing winds.

Having visited Martinsell Hill on many occasions and at all seasons I find that it draws me back time and time again, and I share the feelings of H.W.Timperley when he wrote that he could not recall a single disappointing visit to Martinsell. It is difficult to explain the great affection that has been felt by so many for this hill. The views from it looking both north and south are dramatic, but many other Wiltshire hills offer equally good views and generate that feeling of exhilaration which most of us feel when when we visit high places. For me Martinsell is the supreme hill of all the Wiltshire chalk uplands, and its attraction was probably best expressed by Timperley when he wrote of Martinsell: 'It is a presence and a personality. It is one of those hills that take possession of the imagination from the start, one of the high places that all sorts of people like to visit and revisit or look for in the distance and recognise with pleasurable feelings that may not easily be put into words'.

Since it covers a substantial area about nine miles long by an average of five miles across, and is criss-crossed by a network of public rights of way, Pewsey Vale offers an infinite variety of walking that is practically inexhaustible. The walks that follow are therefore merely an introduction to walking the Vale. From a study of Landranger Map 173, anyone will be able to devise any number of walks in the glorious countryside in and around the Vale of Pewsey.

Suggested Walks in the Vale of Pewsey

The walks in the considerable area of the Vale of Pewsey are virtually endless and the following are offered as a very limited selection.

6A: All Cannings to Tan Hill and Wansdyke (6 miles: map 173):

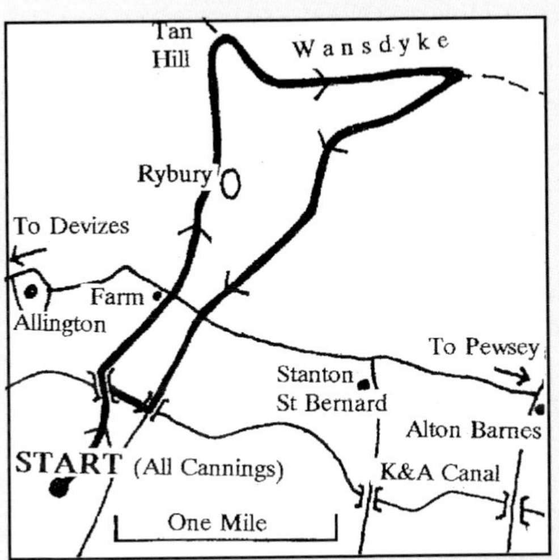

A varied walk from the valley bottom on to the surrounding hills is obtained by walking north from All Cannings, crossing the canal at Woodway Bridge (073624), continuing past All Cannings Farm and mounting the hills along the old track over Clifford's Hill past the twin crests of Rybury which offer tremendous panoramic views. From Rybury the continuation is north to the trig point on Tan Hill which marks both the highest point in Wiltshire (at 964 feet : 294m) and the site of the former Tan Hill Fair which was described in Chapter 3. After following Wansdyke east to Milk Hill (100647) the track running south-west may be followed back to All Cannings (through 085633) under the south-eastern shoulder of Clifford's Hill.

6B: Workway Drove, Wansdyke and the Canal (6.5 miles: map 173):
A walk which offers variety in that it incorporates both downland and waterside walking along the Kennet and Avon Canal towpath is obtained by parking at the Workway Drove car park (116637) under Knap Hill and walking north-west up the Workway Drove to Wansdyke. From a point near where the drove joins Wansdyke a diversion south may be made to see Oxenmere (106641), reputed to be the oldest dewpond in England. Return to Wansdyke and continue west along the dyke, enjoying the magnificent views north over Silbury Hill and Avebury, and south over Salisbury Plain to Old Sarum. The spire of Salisbury Cathedral twenty-three miles away is visible on a clear day. A little before reaching Tan Hill branch (at 100646) left away from Wansdyke down the stone surfaced track which descends down an indent into the escarpment and swings south. During this descent the way forks

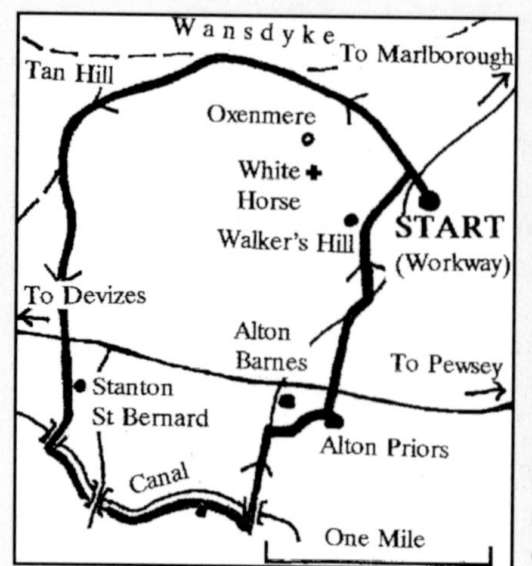

(090638). Be sure to take the left branch. When walking this track several years ago I heard a grasshopper warbler 'churring' from some scrub under the flank of Clifford's Hill. On this descent the Alton White Horse gradually emerges into view to the left along the escarpment from behind Milk Hill. Cross the minor road along the vale (090627) and enter Stanton St Bernard village. After walking to the right (west) of the church and passing Church Farm the canal is soon reached at England's Bridge (090620).

From this bridge the towpath is followed for a mile east to Honey Street where refreshment may be taken at The Barge Inn beside the canal. From the inn continue west along the towpath to the road and then follow the road north with Alton White Horse again visible ahead, turning right to Alton Barnes Saxon church. From the church take the path paved with sarsen sets north-east across a meadow, pass through a turnstile gate left of Alton Priors church, continue through the village, and cross the west to east road along the Vale.

The Ridgeway (111624) – here a hollow way – may then be followed north up the slope. After the Alton to Lockeridge road is crossed at 112629 Adam's Grave long barrow – the most impressively sited long barrow in Wiltshire and perhaps in Wessex – may be visited by climbing the steep slopes over the south face of Walker's Hill. The climb is steep, but the views to the south across the Vale are rewarding. From the top of the hill the starting point in the Workway Drove is visible a few hundred yards to the north-east.

6C: Workway Drove to Martinsell Hill (9 miles: map 173):

An alternative walk that may be followed from the Workway Drove car park (116637) along the north escarpment of Pewsey Vale to Martinsell is achieved by walking east over the north shoulder of Knap Hill and continuing east along the escarpment along the route now known as the Tan Hill Way over Golden Ball Hill, Draycot Hill, north of Gopher Wood, and eastwards over Huish Hill. The Marlborough to Pewsey road is then crossed at 164643 on Oare Hill and the walk is continued south-east and around Martinsell hillfort.

The return is west over the Martinsell plateau, over the Giant's Grave promontory, and descending the steep slope into Oare village where the A345 is again crossed. After passing a little north of Oare House (a fine Georgian house well worth a short diversion) continue westwards by the right of way along a field path to Huish. From near the church at Huish it is possible to climb back up the escarpment past Gopher Wood and return by the outgoing route.

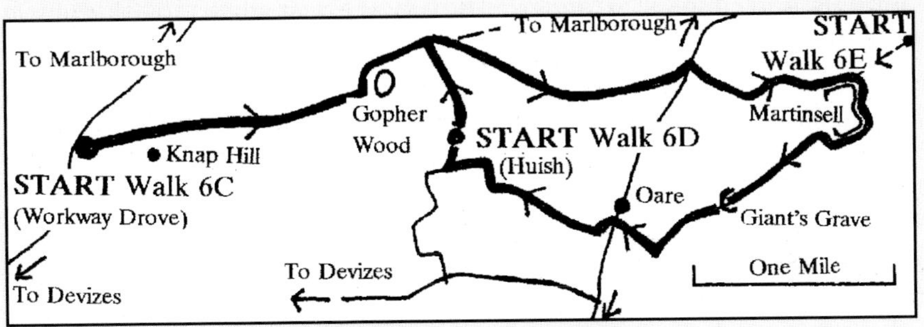

Walks 6C, 6D and 6E

6D: Huish to Martinsell (6 miles: map 173):
Huish church (145637) is another good starting point for walks. The walk from Workway Drove to Martinsell just described may be reduced by about three miles by starting from Huish, although this eliminates the extensive views south from the escarpment between Knap Hill and Gopher Wood.

The approach to Martinsell from the west described above suffers from the disadvantage that it misses the impact that the great bluff of the hill makes when seen from the south or the east, from the direction of the Kennet and Avon Canal or Wootton Rivers in Pewsey Vale, or from Clench Common.

6E: Clench Common over Martinsell to Oare and Huish (7 miles: map 173, see map above):
The best way to approach Martinsell is in my estimation from the east, parking at the car park at 183645 and walking south-west along the south edge of the linear copse which runs towards Martinsell Hill. From this direction the true majesty of the hill can best be appreciated. This was the approach described by Geoffrey Grigson when he wrote: 'But one of the best things about Martinsell is the way to the top, the sweep upwards from the lane at the back of Marlborough, interrupted by the knuckle wind-blown beeches. You have a sense, as you climb, of air, and world, and time'. The ramparts of

the hillfort can be explored, with a continuation south-west to the Giant's Grave over which a footpath descends steeply into Oare village. The dramatic nature of this promontory which led to its folk name and legend can best be appreciated by looking back from Oare. A good circular walk may then be completed by continuing west from Oare along the field footpath to Huish, climbing north from Huish church to the hills near Gopher Wood by an uphill track that can be very muddy. The return route is along the escarpment over Huish Hill and Oare Hill to Martinsell by way of Ravensgate (169641) above Rainscombe.

6F: Cocklebury Farm to Ladies' Bridge and Swanborough Tump
(3 miles; map 173):
Ladies' Bridge and Swanborough Tump may be incorporated in a short walk by parking at Cocklebury Farm (129605), walking the short distance north to Ladies' Bridge, and then following the canal towpath east past Wide Water and Stowell Park (with its cast iron bridge over the canal) to Bristow Bridge.

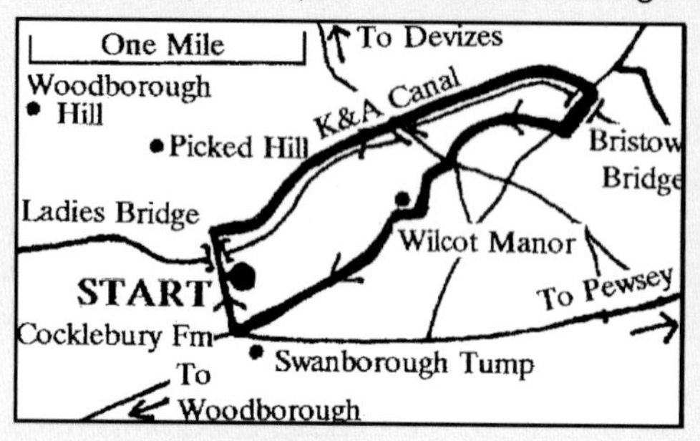

From this bridge the return is by a short walk south-west down the road and then by the field path which leads south-west to Wilcot. After passing through Wilcot branch south-west at the bend south of Wilcot Park (138605) along the footpath which runs directly to Swan-borough Tump beside Frith Wood on the return to Cocklebury.

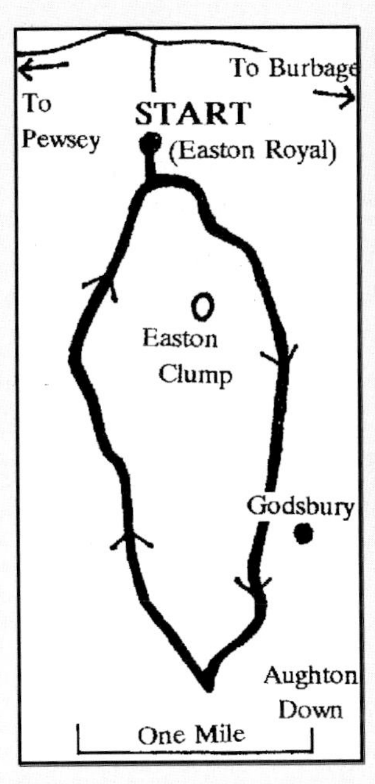

6G: South from Easton Royal over Easton Hill (6 miles: map 174):
South from Easton towards the east end of the Vale more fine downland walking is available around Easton Hill and Clump by taking a four mile walk south-east on to the downs passing west of Crowdown Clump (217577) – formerly known as Godsbury – and continuing to Aughton Down, doubling back at 211566 and returning down the track which runs the west side of Easton Hill to Easton Royal. This is in my experience a good place for wild flowers which are in season often profuse beside these remote downland tracks.

Conclusion

A number of people have told me that by introducing them to walking in rural Wiltshire I have enhanced their lives. In reaching a wider audience with this book I sincerely hope that the experience offered will increase the enjoyment of those who already walk, and persuade them to walk in some of the areas that they do not yet know. It is also my earnest hope that some non-walking readers who chance to pick up this book will try walking as a recreation, and derive from it at least some of the immense enjoyment that walking and researching the history of the Wiltshire landscape have provided for me over more years than I care to remember.

Note

A second volume, *Exploring Historic Wiltshire: Volume 2, South*, in the same format as the present book, is available and covers the following areas shown on the map on page 12:

7 Chute Causeway
8 The Wylye Valley
9 Wiltshire Selwood & White Sheet Downs
10 Great Ridge Wood & Grovely Wood
11 The South Wiltshire Ridgeways
12 South-East Wiltshire

Bibliography

Chapter 1: Ridgeway Country

J.R.L. Anderson and Godwin: *The Oldest Road: An Exploration of the Ridgeway* (Wildwood, 1975)
N. Curtis: *The Ridgeway National Trail Guide* (Aurum, 1989)
E. Thomas: *The Icknield Way* (Chapter 1) (Nelson, 1914)
E. Thomas: *Richard Jefferies: His Life and Work* (Chapter 1) (Hutchinson, 1908)
H.W Timperley: *Ridge Way Country* (Batsford, 1935)
K. Watts: *The Marlborough Downs* (Ex Libris Press, 1993)
K. Watts: *Snap* (Wiltshire County Council, 1989)
A. Williams: *Villages of the White Horse* (Duckworth, 1913)

Chapter 2 : The Central Marlborough Downs

H.C. Brentnall and Carter: *The Marlborough Country* (Oxford, 1932)
E. Thomas: *Richard Jefferies: His Life and Work* Chapter 1) (Hutchinson, 1908)
K. Watts: *The Marlborough Downs* (Ex Libris Press, 1993)
Wiltshire Archaeological Magazine (Volume 58)

Chapter 3: Wansdyke

J. Chandler: *The Vale of Pewsey* (Ex Libris Press, 1991)
O.G.S. Crawford: *Archaeology in the Field* (Appendix 4) (Phoenix, 1953)
H.W. Timperley: *The Vale of Pewsey* (Hale, 1954)
K. Watts : *The Marlborough Downs* (Ex Libris Press, 1993).

Chapter 4 : Grigson Country

G. Grigson: *The Crest on the Silver* (1950)
G. Grigson: *Recollections* (1984)
As there are few publications on this area readers may wish to refer to the *Victoria County History of Wiltshire* (Volume 9) and the *Wiltshire Archaeological Magazines* (particularly Volume 44)

Chapter 5: Calstone, Oldbury and Roundway Down

O.G.S. Crawford: *Archaeology in the Field* (Chapter 7) (Phoenix, 1953)
I. Gandy: *Round About the Little Steeple* (Allen & Unwin, 1960)
D. Philip: *The Great Bath Road* (Countryside Books, 1983)
Col. H.C.B. Rogers: *Battles and Generals of the Civil War* (Seeley Service, 1968)

Chapter 6: The Vale of Pewsey

J. Chandler: *The Vale of Pewsey* (Ex Libris Press, 1991)
I. Gandy: *Round About the Little Steeple* (Allen & Unwin, 1960)
H.W. Timperley: *The Vale of Pewsey* (Hale, 1954)
B. Vesey-Fitzgerald: *The Hampshire Avon* (Cassell, 1950)

Index – Illustrations referred to in bold